T0339727

Cambridge Elements ≡

Elements in Politics and Society in Latin America
edited by
Maria Victoria Murillo
Columbia University
Tulia G. Falleti
University of Pennsylvania
Juan Pablo Luna
The Pontifical Catholic University of Chile
Andrew Schrank
Brown University

INNOVATING DEMOCRACY?

The Means and Ends of Citizen Participation in Latin America

Thamy Pogrebinschi
WZB Berlin Social Science Center

CAMBRIDGE
UNIVERSITY PRESS

Shaftesbury Road, Cambridge CB2 8EA, United Kingdom

One Liberty Plaza, 20th Floor, New York, NY 10006, USA

477 Williamstown Road, Port Melbourne, VIC 3207, Australia

314–321, 3rd Floor, Plot 3, Splendor Forum, Jasola District Centre,
New Delhi – 110025, India

103 Penang Road, #05–06/07, Visioncrest Commercial, Singapore 238467

Cambridge University Press is part of Cambridge University Press & Assessment,
a department of the University of Cambridge.

We share the University's mission to contribute to society through the pursuit of
education, learning and research at the highest international levels of excellence.

www.cambridge.org
Information on this title: www.cambridge.org/9781108712880

DOI: 10.1017/9781108690010

© Thamy Pogrebinschi 2023

This publication is in copyright. Subject to statutory exception and to the provisions
of relevant collective licensing agreements, no reproduction of any part may take
place without the written permission of Cambridge University Press & Assessment.

First published 2023

A catalogue record for this publication is available from the British Library.

ISBN 978-1-108-71288-0 Paperback
ISSN 2515-5253 (online)
ISSN 2515-5245 (print)

Cambridge University Press & Assessment has no responsibility for the persistence
or accuracy of URLs for external or third-party internet websites referred to in this
publication and does not guarantee that any content on such websites is, or will
remain, accurate or appropriate.

Innovating Democracy?

The Means and Ends of Citizen Participation in Latin America

Elements in Politics and Society in Latin America

DOI: 10.1017/9781108690010
First published online: April 2023

Thamy Pogrebinschi
WZB Berlin Social Science Center
Author for correspondence: Thamy Pogrebinschi, thamy.pogrebinschi@wzb.eu

Abstract: Since democratization, Latin America has experienced a surge in new forms of citizen participation. Yet there is still little comparative knowledge on these so-called democratic innovations. This Element seeks to fill this gap. Drawing on a new dataset with 3,744 cases from 18 countries between 1990 and 2020, it presents the first large-N cross-country study of democratic innovations to date. It also introduces a typology of twenty kinds of democratic innovations, which are based on four means of participation, namely deliberation, citizen representation, digital engagement, and direct voting. Adopting a pragmatist, problem-driven approach, this Element claims that democratic innovations seek to enhance democracy by addressing public problems through combinations of these four means of participation in pursuit of one or more of five ends of innovations, namely accountability, responsiveness, rule of law, social equality, and political inclusion.

Keywords: citizen participation, Latin America, civil society, democracy, democratic innovations

© Thamy Pogrebinschi 2023

ISBNs: 9781108712880 (PB), 9781108690010 (OC)
ISSNs: 2515-5253 (online), 2515-5245 (print)

For Hannah,
because women can be mothers and write books.

Contents

1 Introduction

Democracy in Latin America has been challenged in recent years. In 2018 the downgrading of Venezuela and Nicaragua to autocracies led Latinobarómetro to call that an *annus horribilis* (terrible year) for democracy in the region (Lagos, 2018: 1), and the political landscape has only further deteriorated since. At least three other countries have flirted with some form of authoritarianism, namely, Brazil, El Salvador, and Haiti. Bolivia saw a president forced to resign by the military, Peru had three presidents within a single week, Haiti was left without president after the incumbent was murdered, Mexico's president called a national referendum to prosecute his predecessors, and Nicaragua held presidential elections without political competition. At the same time, and despite a deadly pandemic that required social distancing, citizens have taken to the streets in nearly all countries of the region. In Colombia and Nicaragua, they were brutally repressed by the police. In a Guatemala washed by hurricanes, however, their actions led to suspension of a budget that cut health spending. And in Chile, they managed to elect the world's first gender-parity constitutional assembly.

The COVID-19 outbreak in 2020 made things even more complicated. It tested the resilience of political institutions and the limits of state capacity, while also deepening long-standing problems such as political instability, economic crisis, and social inequality. Dissatisfaction with democracy has risen to 70 percent, "deepening the crisis of representation" in the region (Latinobarómetro, 2021: 8). Nonetheless, while at the onset of the pandemic scholars were concerned that elections and protests would diminish with the spread of the virus and hence undermine Latin America's main mechanisms of accountability (Murillo, 2020), with some delay almost all planned elections were held, and citizens have protested everywhere evidencing a demand for further democratic legitimacy (Murillo, 2021).

Civil society's role was nonetheless "not simply confined to being the locus of protest," since civil society organizations (CSOs) have played a critical role in alleviating the impacts of the pandemic and an "explosion of civic activism" was felt also in other arenas (International IDEA, 2021: 34 and 11). Those arenas are institutions, processes, and mechanisms of citizen participation that have spread across Latin America over more than three decades: the so-called democratic innovations.

After most of Latin America transitioned to democracy in the late 1980s, many countries began to experiment with new institutional designs that included citizens and CSOs in the policy cycle. The flagship of what only later became known as "democratic innovations" was participatory budgeting, introduced in Porto Alegre, Brazil, in late 1989. This process of enabling citizens to set expenditure priorities for local governments quickly spread to hundreds of cities across Latin America. Its success stemmed not only from its initial achievements in terms of inclusion and equality (Abers, 1998) but also from the fact that it demonstrated that citizens can indeed play a role in the policy process and may thereby improve democracy (Wampler & Goldfrank, 2022).

While participatory budgeting became undoubtedly the most well-known democratic innovation created in Latin America since the third wave of democracy landed on the region's shores, it is far from the only one – let alone the most impactful one. Since 1990, the region has undergone a prolific surge in new forms of participation beyond elections, associations, and protests. Thousands of different participatory institutions, processes, and mechanisms have emerged throughout nearly all Latin American countries. In some of them, the adoption of participatory institutions became mandatory, especially at the subnational level (McNulty, 2019). Altogether, democratic innovations have engaged millions of citizens and mobilized thousands of CSOs, in addition to having impacted hundreds of public policies at the national and subnational levels.

Although their relevance for a comprehensive account of democracy in Latin America is undisputable, these institutions, processes, and mechanisms of citizen participation are still little known, especially outside of the countries where they took root. With few notable exceptions, international scholarship has focused mostly on participatory budgeting. Fewer works have been devoted to other institutions such as, for example, housing councils (Donaghy, 2013), water management councils (Abers & Keck, 2013), community-managed schools (Altschuler & Corrales, 2013), national public policy conferences (Pogrebinschi & Samuels, 2014), health councils (Falleti & Cunial, 2018), prior consultations (Falleti & Riofrancos, 2018), planning councils (Mayka, 2019), and development councils (McNulty, 2019). Regardless of the immense contributions made by these and other works, existing research consists mostly of case studies of local-level participatory institutions, which are seldom comparative, and therefore provides just a partial account of democratic experimentation with citizen participation in Latin America.

Without the full picture, many questions remain unanswered, and the roles of these participatory innovations in democracy in Latin America remain understudied. What is innovative about so-called democratic innovations? What kinds of participation do they entail? Why have these participatory innovations evolved in Latin America? What types of democratic innovations exist, and how diverse are they across countries? These are only a few of the many questions that cannot be answered by case studies of individual, small-scale participatory institutions.

I tackle these questions by providing a comprehensive account of democratic experimentation with citizen participation in Latin America over thirty years. I present the first large-N cross-country study of democratic innovations to date. It draws on my own original dataset that comprises 3,744 institutions, processes, and mechanisms of citizen participation implemented at both national and subnational levels in 18 countries in the region between 1990 and 2020 (Pogrebinschi, 2021a). The Innovations for Democracy in Latin America (LATINNO) dataset, whose methodology will be presented in the next section, is the first systematic endeavor to map, measure, and compare a large number of democratic innovations across Latin America.

I make three contributions to comparative politics and democratic theory. First, I introduce a pragmatist, problem-driven approach to democratic innovations, which challenges the conventional understanding that such innovations are primarily designed to increase citizen participation in decision-making. Countering this common understanding, I claim that citizen participation is not an end in itself and that democratic innovations are not merely designed to increase it. Instead, I argue that citizen participation is a *means* to achieve an end, namely the enhancement of democracy. Relying on the LATINNO data, I contend that democratic innovations that have evolved in Latin America in the last thirty years have not been designed simply to increase the number of citizens who participate in policy processes. Their purpose has rather been to enhance democracy by addressing specific problems that hinder it, and to do so *by means of* citizen participation.

Grounded in the data and pragmatism's assumption that "problem-solving refers to collective processes in which the settings of ends and the devising of means are inextricably intertwined" (Frega, 2019: 19), I argue that the democratic innovations that evolved in Latin America between 1990 and 2020 disclose four primary *means* of citizen participation, namely deliberation, citizen representation, digital engagement, and direct voting. I claim that those means of participation in democratic innovations combine with different *ends* according to the problem(s) they seek to address. Based on an examination of the design of democratic innovations and their stated aims, I contend that those *ends* are accountability, responsiveness, rule of law, social equality, and political inclusion.

While those five ends of democratic innovations have been inferred from the 3,744 cases in the LATINNO dataset, they reflect some known dimensions of measurements of the quality of democracy, or what Morlino (2011) calls "democratic qualities." I claim that democratic innovations aim to enhance democracy by seeking to enhance at least one of its five dimensions or "qualities." The five ends serve thus as criteria against which further studies may assess the impact of democratic innovations on the quality of democracy. I conceptualize the means and ends as "data containers" (Sartori, 2009 [1975]), that is, defined and categorized empirical facts. Hence, the ends do not reflect a set of functions or normative values. Instead, my pragmatic approach relies on the empirical reciprocal determination of means of citizen participation and ends of democratic innovations. Drawing on the data, I show that democratic innovations have been designed over the last thirty years combining the four means and five ends with one another depending on the problems each specific design has explicitly intended to address. I identify the most frequent problems related to each of the five ends, suggesting that they can be related to three known challenges faced by democracy in Latin America: deficits of representation, (un)rule of law, and inequality.

Second, I propose the first typology of democratic innovations based on a large-N dataset of cases evolved at both national and subnational levels across eighteen countries for a period of thirty years. Previous attempts to classify democratic innovations relied on literature review or on a small number of case studies originating mostly from the global North (Smith, 2009; Geissel, 2013; Elstub & Escobar, 2019). Drawing on 3,744 cases from Latin America, my typology uses the four means of participation (deliberation, citizen representation, digital engagement, and direct voting) as categorical variables that enable the differentiation of 20 subtypes of democratic innovations. Typologies are crucial for comparative research, as well as for rigorous concept formation and measurement (Collier & Levitsky, 2009). Classifying democratic innovations based on their designs is essential for making them comparable and for enabling conceptual clarity, that is, refining the concept of democratic innovation by increasing analytical differentiation. Moreover, the twenty subtypes of democratic innovations devised in my typology reflect "a menu of institutional alternatives" that can "serve to guide and discipline efforts to improve the quality of democratic governance" (Fung, 2012: 614). The diversity of institutional designs that I present in this Element can hopefully contribute to altering the diagnosis that the field of democratic innovations has been built predominantly around studies of participatory budgeting (Ryan, 2021).

I also seek to analytically refine the concept of democratic innovations, proposing a definition that is based on both a large-N set of cases and on empirical evidence from the global South, that is, from Latin America. I take issue with the specialized literature to claim that democratic innovations are not restricted to participatory institutions. Instead, I argue that there are three kinds of democratic innovations, namely institutions, processes, and mechanisms.

I also oppose the view that democratic innovations are state-sanctioned institutions, and rather I claim that civil society and international organizations (as well as private stakeholders) are also promoters of democratic innovations. Moreover, I call into question the assumption, present in established definitions (Smith, 2009), that democratic innovations are designed to increase citizen participation in decision-making processes. Alternatively, I claim that there are four moments of innovation and that citizen participation, regardless of whether it results in a political decision, can take place in all four stages of the policy cycle, namely agenda-setting, policy formulation, implementation, and evaluation. Taking these empirical aspects into account, I define democratic innovations as institutions, processes, and mechanisms whose end it is to enhance democracy by means of citizen participation in at least one stage of the policy cycle.

Third, I offer a comparative account of democratic experimentation with citizen participation in Latin America from 1990 to 2020. I argue that five aspects facilitated the creation of democratic innovations in the region, namely democratization, constitutionalization, decentralization, the left turn, and digitalization. I do not claim that these are the causes of or necessary conditions for the implementation of democratic innovations. Rather, these aspects indicate a favorable context specifically found in Latin America throughout the three decades studied in which democratic innovations grew in the region. The analysis of cases created each year across eighteen countries over the thirty years discloses, among other things, a trend I discuss in the conclusion of this Element: since the end of the left turn around 2015, deliberation promoted by governments has decreased in Latin America, while digital engagement advanced by civil society indicates a new path for democratic innovation in the region.

While the large-N cross-country study presented in this Element fills a gap in a field dominated by case studies of few democratic innovations which are seldom of a comparative nature, large-N comparative research is not free of shortcomings. This becomes clear in the analysis of impact that I present in Section 5. While a categorization of means and ends of 3,744 democratic innovations in 18 countries is only feasible through a documentary analysis of their designs and stated goals, the assessment of innovations' impact (e.g., the extent to which their ends are achieved) is limited by lack of available qualitative evidence, which results in many missing pieces of information.

The pragmatist approach to democratic innovations introduced in this Element builds on concepts originated from pragmatist philosophy, in particular John Dewey. A problem-solving approach grounded in the interaction of means and ends is one of the basic tenets of Dewey's thought. Scholars who applied pragmatism to democracy converge on the centrality of an experimental process of institutional innovation aimed at solving problems (Knight & Johnson, 2011; Frega, 2019) and pursuing what Dewey called "ends-in-view" (1938), which would "push people to develop creative strategies for problem solving" (Ansell, 2011: 84), "motivate democratic reform efforts" (Fung, 2012: 611), and ultimately lead to "radical reform as a species of transformative politics" (Unger, 1998:18).

Democratic experimentalism, however, entails not only institutional innovation as problem solving aimed at achieving desirable consequences, but also underscores fallibility and revisability as important aspects of democracy. This makes pragmatism an even more suitable perspective to analyze democratic innovations, especially in Latin America. Latin America's democratic experimentalism, or what I earlier called the region's pragmatic democracy (Pogrebinschi, 2013; Pogrebinschi, 2018), illustrates well both a continuous process of experimentation with institutional designs and its inherent tentative and fallible nature. While thousands of democratic innovations have been designed in the region to address various important public problems, they have many times failed to solve those very problems. Likewise, the democratic ends purportedly pursued by democratic innovations may sometimes prove to be just a window-dressing strategy. Nonetheless, this does not imply that the institutions, processes, and mechanisms of citizen participation are any less valuable for democracy – especially in a region where the main institutions of representative democracy are themselves routinely deemed flawed or defective.

This Element is organized in six sections, including this introduction. Section 2 presents the data on which this Element draws, painting the empirical landscape that supports the claims made throughout. After explaining the methodology behind the data, I discuss five aspects that played a role on the experimentation with democratic innovations in Latin America between 1990 and 2020. Section 3 presents the concept of democratic innovation that lies at the core of the analysis contained in this Element. It engages with the specialized scholarship and relies on empirical data in order to argue that citizen participation is a means of innovation, and not its end. Section 4 proposes a typology of democratic innovations based on the four means of participation – deliberation, citizen representation, digital engagement, and direct voting – that have evolved in Latin America since 1990. I briefly introduce each of the twenty subtypes of democratic innovations that can be distinguished across the region. Section 5 expands on the problem-driven nature of democratic innovations, relating the problems that innovations seek to address with five interrelated ends: accountability, responsiveness, rule of law, social equality, and political inclusion. This section also depicts how means and ends combine to address concrete problems and presents data on the impact of democratic innovations. The sixth and final section claims that regardless of their inability to hinder recent democratic backslides in Latin America, democratic innovations, as the utmost expression of the region's democratic experimentalism, have been crucial in calling attention to new ways of addressing public problems through citizen participation. It also points out recent trends in the data that reveal possible directions that democratic innovation might take in the future.

2 The Empirical Landscape

Democratic innovations have been expanding in Latin America since the end of the twentieth century. During the 1990s, they were pushed by democratization, constitutional lawmaking, and decentralization processes. With the new century, the left turn was the main trigger of democratic innovation, with left-leaning political parties unleashing a new wave of institutions, processes, and mechanisms that sought to include citizens in policymaking. After 2010, but especially since 2015, as most left governments lost power, digitalization has increasingly played a crucial role, strengthening civil society and potentially starting a new era of democratic innovation in Latin America, one in which the state no longer holds the reins in the expansion of citizen participation.

This section presents the empirical landscape on which this Element is grounded. It traces the expansion of democratic innovations in Latin America between 1990 and 2020, while arguing that five overlapping aspects have created a favorable context to citizen participation. Building such a narrative, which is not linear for all eighteen countries, allows me to introduce the data upon which my overall analysis is based. I start by explaining the methodology behind the LATINNO dataset.

2.1 Comparing Democratic Innovations

I designed the LATINNO dataset with the intention of compiling measurable and comparable data on democratic innovations in Latin America, which could provide empirical answers to contemporary debates on political theory and comparative politics regarding the role of citizen participation in democracy. The dataset is the main result of an almost six-year research project (2015–2021), which involved thirty-two research assistants under my coordination.[1] It comprises 3,744 democratic innovations implemented between 1990 and 2020 in 18 countries, namely Argentina, Brazil, Bolivia, Chile, Colombia, Costa

---

[1] All data can be browsed in the project's website (www.latinno.net), and the full dataset is available at the SowiDataNet/datorium data repositorium (https://doi.org/10.7802/2278). See Pogrebinschi 2021a.

Rica, Dominican Republic, Ecuador, El Salvador, Guatemala, Honduras, Mexico, Nicaragua, Paraguay, Panama, Peru, Uruguay, and Venezuela.[2]

The LATINNO dataset was built considering single cases of democratic innovations as the independent variable. It relied on a specific concept of democratic innovation and my pragmatist analytical framework, both of which will be discussed in later sections. Democratic innovations were defined according to three criteria, all of which had to be matched for an innovation to be considered democratic and hence included as a case in the dataset:

(1) Citizen Participation: Democratic innovations must involve citizen engagement, which can take any form that fits the definition of one (or more) of four means of participation, namely, deliberation, citizen representation, direct voting, and digital engagement.
(2) Democracy Enhancement: Democratic innovations must be designed with the aim to enhance democracy, addressing one (or more) of five ends, namely accountability, responsiveness, rule of law, social equality, and political inclusion.
(3) Impact on Policy Cycle: Democratic innovations must be designed in such a way as to enable citizens and/or civil society organizations (CSOs) to engage in one (or more) stages of the policy cycle, namely: agenda setting, formulation, implementation, and evaluation.

The LATINNO dataset was built after a pilot project during which an initial collection of about 350 cases from six countries enabled the refinement of both the dataset's analytical unit (democratic innovations) and framework (means of participation and ends of innovations). As it shall become clearer in Section 4, I understand those concepts as "data containers" (Sartori, 2009 [1975]), that is, refined empirical facts that have been quantitatively and qualitatively defined and categorized. Although I departed from democratic theory (scholarship on participation, deliberation, and democratic innovations) and comparative politics (literature on quality of democracy and Latin America's politics and society) to frame the working concepts and analytical framework, it was only after this pilot stage that, based on the initial empirical evidence collected, I refined the definitions that oriented the search and identification of cases (in particular, those of means and ends), as well as the variables that compose the codebook (see Pogrebinschi, 2021b). As more data for a larger number of countries were collected throughout the three stages of the project (see Pogrebinschi, 2021c:15), I continued to further refine concepts and update variables until

---

[2] The initial idea was to include all twenty independent countries of Latin America, but research in Cuba and Haiti has proven difficult, and the absence of enough and reliable data for those two countries implied leaving them aside to ensure the general comparability of the dataset.

after the first version of the dataset was released in mid-2017. This continuous work – from concepts to empirical evidence and back – aimed to improve the accuracy and hence the validity of the data, as well as ensure that the dataset's analytical framework was grounded in empirical evidence and not in normative concepts.

My definition of democratic innovations as *institutions, processes, and mechanisms whose end it is to enhance democracy by means of citizen partici-pation in at least one stage of the policy cycle* has thus resulted from the very process of construction of the dataset. It was only after the first version of the dataset was completed that it became clear from the empirical evidence col-lected, for example, that democratic innovations were of three distinct kinds, namely, institutions, processes, and mechanisms. The framing of such evidence-based classification led to the posterior insertion of a new variable (kind of innovation) in the codebook and the recoding of all cases to include this additional information. Another example of this method of going back and forth between concepts and data was the inclusion of rule of law as the fifth end of innovations. It was only after the accumulation of a significant number of potential cases whose design aimed at engaging citizens in matters of, for example, law enforcement, conflict resolution, peace processes, public security, and protection of human rights, that I decided to include this category in the codebook and have the respective body of empirical evidence coded and integrated into the dataset.

In order to ensure comparability across cases, all three criteria comprised in the concept of democratic innovations had to be simultaneously present in each case included in the dataset. Hence, evidence of participatory practices that did not match the other two criteria (democracy enhancement and impact on policy cycle) was discarded. This implied leaving out of the dataset several initiatives (for example, hundreds of CSO projects devoted to developing citizens' polit-ical skills or to empower groups) simply because they lacked an institutional design potentially able to impact the policy cycle or had no clear goal to improve democracy. Likewise, initiatives explicitly designed to enhance dem-ocracy and have an impact on public policies were discarded if there was no actual citizen participation involved. That happened to some initiatives carried out only by the staff of a CSO, without actual engagement of the citizenry.

The choice of criteria for case selection also ensured the "democratic" character of innovations included in the dataset. The aim was not to collect all kinds of participatory experiences (i.e., those that simply include citizens), but rather only those that by design explicitly sought to enhance democracy by improving at least one of the five ends. According with these criteria, the dataset includes innovations implemented in countries that were downgraded to dictatorships (such as Nicaragua and Venezuela in 2018). The specialized scholarship has demonstrated how democratic innovations in authoritarian countries may strengthen authoritarian rule or serve as a leading edge of democratization (He & Warren, 2011). Keeping track of those cases is relevant for this reason, and also to understand the role of civil society in opposing authoritarianism through participatory innovations.

The LATINNO dataset aims to reveal and underscore the diversity of institutional designs of democratic innovations across Latin America, instead of compiling a full inventory of every place where the same democratic innovation has been implemented within all eighteen countries. Given that several participatory institutions have been adopted across thousands of municipalities within a single country (for instance, health councils in Brazil and development councils in Guatemala) or hundreds of times within a single city (for instance, community councils in Caracas, Venezuela), it would be impossible to retrieve information for each existing case, much less to cover so many countries (eighteen) over a long period of time (thirty years). Thus, I chose to prioritize the diversity of institutional designs, and only differentiate similar cases within single countries when the rules according to which an institution, process, or mechanism was organized were indeed different.

Hence, the dataset does not include, for example, local health councils implemented in each of Brazil's 5,570 cities as separate cases in the aggregate data, but as a single instance in the Brazil subdataset. As for participatory institutions with similar institutional designs but relevant differences in their conception and organization (for instance, Brazil's national public policy conferences on diverse policy areas), cases have been coded separately. Individual coding has also been done for similar participatory institutions (such as referenda, plebiscites, or popular recalls) that have not been adopted or implemented too many times within single countries. The number of replications of a given democratic innovation within a country was assigned in a specific variable.

Each democratic innovation included in the dataset has been carefully described and coded for forty-three variables designed to understand the innovation's context, institutional design, and impact. These variables were initially developed in the pilot stage of the project based on their theoretical interest and were gradually adjusted to better reflect the empirical data. *Context variables* capture the place and moment in which democratic innovations were first created, their duration, the political parties involved, and their ideological orientation. *Institutional design variables* reflect formal features of democratic innovations, such as who created them, the type of participants and how they were selected, the level and scope of implementation, the extent to which they were institutionalized and allowed to yield decisions, the means employed, the ends pursued, the policy issues dealt with, and the stages of the policy cycle affected. Finally, *impact variables* assess the actual implementation of democratic innovations, whether they were really carried out and, if so, how many times/in how many places they took place, the number of participants involved, the extent to which they fulfilled their aims and had an impact on their ends, and whether outputs (results) and outcomes (policies) ensued.

Institutional design variables have been mostly coded according to de jure attributes of democratic innovations. This was necessary given the scope of the dataset. Only legislation, policies, official documents, or materials related to the creation or functioning of a democratic innovation can provide a description of an institutional design that may be replicated with distinct de facto attributes depending on when and where it is adopted within a country. Impact variables, on the other hand, have been coded using de facto information, that is, existing and reliable qualitative assessments (such as scholarly work, case studies, impact reports). Given that some democratic innovations are replicated numerous times within countries, coders relied on all available reliable evidence of impact, which many times included mixed evidence from different places or moments where one same design has been implemented. Hence, while the variable "ends" has been coded based on an analysis of the goals reflected on and inferred from the design of the innovation, the variable "impact on ends" has been coded according to evidence originated from diverse reliable sources that provided a qualitative evaluation of the innovation in question.

The five "ends" of innovations echo dimensions employed by scholarship on quality of democracy and indicators used by democracy indexes to measure the quality of democracies (see Section 5.1). In the pilot stage of the construction of the dataset, the goals stated in the first 350 cases collected were analyzed according to Morlino's (2011) eight "democratic qualities" (and their respective indicators), resulting in the identification of five recurring ends. The ends reflect thus dimensions of democracy aimed at improvement, which can also be inferred from the problems innovations are designed to tackle. By expanding and adapting five of Morlino's democratic qualities in face of the empirical evidence, I created indicators used to code the variable "ends" (see LATINNO Codebook, Pogrebinschi, 2021b).

Democratic innovations were sought, identified, and coded according to an extensive list of sources that has been adapted to each specific country. This list included academic literature and research reports; national and subnational legislation; governmental institutions, civil society organizations, international organizations; existing databanks, data pools, and impact assessments; political parties, politicians, activists, scholars, and the national and local media. The case search for each country was considered concluded only after coders reached a stage of data exhaustion, that is, after they had gone through all sources and did not find any more cases.

In order to ensure the reliability of the data, all LATINNO's research assistants underwent intensive training before they started to search for and code cases. Throughout the project, inter-reliability tests were taken, coders were closely monitored, and the coded cases were reviewed by me or senior team members. All 3,744 cases of the dataset were fully documented in individual digital files, which contained the entire material collected for each democratic innovation from all sources consulted, including legislation, policies, institutional documents, government websites, articles, and impact reports. In addition to coding each case according to the codebook in an Excel file, coders simultaneously filled out a digital form justifying some of their coding choices and providing supporting evidence.

The LATINNO dataset was expanded, reviewed, and updated several times by diverse subteams of coders until the project's completion in mid-2021. As a final step to assure the validity and reliability of the data, all data and metadata have been checked for consistency and accuracy by the Research Data Management Team at the WZB Berlin Social Sciences Center.

2.2 The Expansion of Democratic Innovations in Latin America

The LATINNO data depict the landscape of democratic innovations in Latin America between 1990 and 2020, providing a broad narrative of how citizen participation has expanded in the region since democratization. Of the 3,744 cases in the dataset, the analysis contained in this Element left aside democratic innovations implemented at the transnational level (involving more than one country), reducing the universe to 3,713 cases distributed across the 18 countries as pictured in Figure 1.[3]

While most innovations are concentrated in South America, pushed by Argentina and Brazil in their struggles to overcome authoritarianism and long periods governed by the left, Colombia and Mexico stand out as countries with a tradition of institutionalizing democratic innovations propelled first by legislation and later by digitalization. While one could expect larger and more populous countries to adopt a higher number of democratic innovations, small countries such as Ecuador and Uruguay make clear how country-specific factors may play a critical role in the development of democratic innovations.

---

[3] This figure displays the totals of democratic innovations created in each country between 1990 and 2020 irrespective of their duration. It also includes democratic innovations created before 1990 which have subsequently undergone significant institutional change.

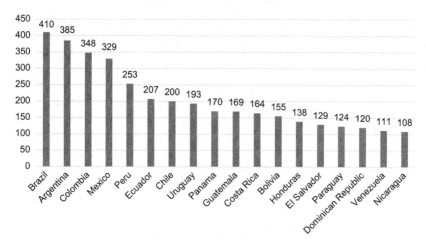

Figure 1 Total number of democratic innovations across countries

Given its long history of political conflict and social unrest, Central America has a weaker tradition of citizen participation, but its comparatively lower number of democratic innovations is somehow offset by their wide replication at the local level. In Guatemala, a country that undertook decentralization later than others, over 12,819 participatory development councils were implemented at the community level by 2010. In Honduras, over 5,000 water boards have been adopted since 2006 to enable citizens to self-manage systems of potable water and sewage.

At least five aspects created a favorable context for democratic innovations to grow in Latin America between 1990 and 2020: democratization, constitutionalization, decentralization, the left turn, and digitalization. Although each of these aspects has prevailed in a specific period of time, they interplay and overlap in different moments and countries. Democratization, constitutionalization, and decentralization were closely connected in several countries in the 1990s and 2000s, enabling the number of democratic innovations created each year to rise steadily in the region, as shown in Figure 2.[4] After the turn of the century, the left turn intensified the expansion of democratic innovations, with left-leaning governments pushing the number of new designs created per year to reach a peak in 2015. The end of the left turn brought about the decline of both state-led and deliberative democratic innovations after 2015, which made room for digitalization to facilitate a new context where democratic innovation is mostly led by civil society, as became clear during the COVID-19 pandemic in 2020.

---

[4] This graph excludes seventy-seven democratic innovations created before 1990 (which, however, underwent significant institutional change after that)

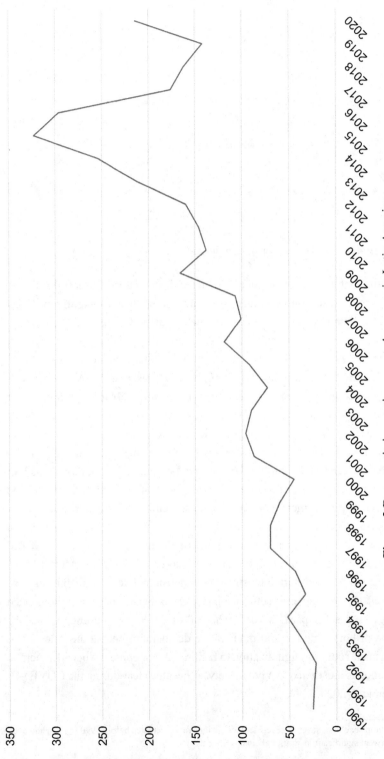

Figure 2 Democratic innovations created per year in Latin America

Starting in the 1990s, democratization was the initial impulse that led to the creation of new forms of citizen participation in Latin America. In order to forgo authoritarianism, various political institutions were redesigned to make room for civil society (for example, in commissions, committees, and boards created within the Executive branch). As a result of their transitions, several Latin American countries underwent a process of constitutional reform and participation was incorporated into new legal orders that devised numerous participatory institutions. Between 1990 and 1999, a total of 436 new designs for citizen participation were created across all countries. Governments were involved in the creation of 85 percent of these democratic innovations, most of which institutions that combined deliberation and citizen representation. Half (51 percent) of the new institutional designs were councils of some sort, namely deliberative, representative, or management councils that were set up at the national and subnational levels in almost equal numbers. About 41 percent of these democratic innovations dealt with issues related to social policy, one-third of which concerned health and education. Mechanisms of direct voting were inscribed in several constitutions but amounted to no more than 12 percent of the new designs conceived in that decade.

Countries with very different political contexts such as Brazil, Bolivia, Colombia, and Ecuador enacted legislation promoting citizen participation and creating participatory institutions during the 1990s. In some countries pro-participation lawmaking was a protection against authoritarianism, but in others it was a consequence of neoliberal policies. While in Brazil the wide adoption of participatory institutions can be linked to the democratizing role of the 1988 "citizen constitution" and ensuing legislation, Colombia's 1991 constitution (comprising 65 articles specifying participatory institutions) and 1994 Participation Law came into effect in a neoliberal context. Figure 3 indicates that these two countries created the highest number of democratic innovations in the 1990s. In Brazil, numerous participatory councils were created at both national and subnational levels in the years following the enactment of the new constitution. In Colombia, dozens of councils, committees, and commissions at all levels were created, especially after the Participation Law was passed.

Decentralization was another aspect that created a favorable context for the expansion of democratic innovations in Latin America. In the 1990s in some countries and in the 2000s in others, decentralization laws promoted participation or were followed by specific legislation conceiving new designs for citizen participation at the local level. Countries that never really embraced democratic innovation, such as Panama and Paraguay, only advanced citizen participation following the enactment of decentralization laws in 2015 and 2010, respectively. While altogether no more than 57 percent of democratic innovations

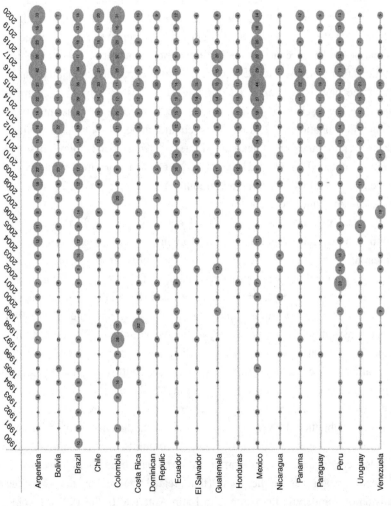

Figure 3 Democratic innovations created per year across countries

created in Latin America over the thirty years took place at the subnational level, within single countries as many as 794 of them were implemented in between 2 and 100 different localities, 120 between 101 and 1,000, and 67 designs were replicated in more than 1,000 places (which includes provinces, cities, districts, etc.).

The impact of decentralization on democratic innovation is quite clear, for example, in Costa Rica, Guatemala, and Peru, as depicted in Figure 3. In Costa Rica, dozens of participatory institutions were created at the subnational level after the enactment of decentralization laws in 1998 and 2010. In Guatemala, two laws passed in 2002 – the General Decentralization Law and the Law on Urban and Rural Development Councils – ensured the participation of citizens in dozens of institutions replicated at the regional, departmental, municipal, and communal levels. More than half of the democratic innovations created in Guatemala in that year involved international organizations in their implementation, an indication of the role played by the international development agenda in the expansion of democratic innovation at the subnational level. In Peru after the removal of Fujimori in late 2000, numerous participatory institutions such as committees, councils, and deliberative tables were created and further expanded to the subnational level in the context of decentralization reforms pushed by newly elected President Alejandro Toledo, which culminated in a Law on Decentralization enacted in 2002. One-fifth of all participatory designs implemented in Peru over the three decades were created solely between 2001 and 2003.

After the turn of the century, the left turn enabled extensive experimentation with citizen participation until the first half of the 2010s. Although parties from all political ideologies launched new forms of citizen participation in Latin America, democratic innovation was quite intense during the considerably shorter time the left spent leading national governments. Exactly half of the 2,209 democratic innovations created between 2000 and 2015 in the region came to life under left governments. Countries like Ecuador and El Salvador mostly implemented democratic innovations while left governments were in office. Bolivia and Chile created significantly more designs for citizen participation while governed by the left. In Brazil, a country with a long tradition of state-led citizen participation, 67 percent of democratic innovations created by governments were implemented with the Workers' Party in power. In Uruguay, the country that was longest governed by the left, 74 percent of democratic innovations were implemented under the Broad Front.

The left enabled participation to scale up to the national level. Between 2008 and 2015, when the left was in power in around two-thirds of countries in Latin

America, left parties were responsible for 87 percent of democratic innovations created by governments at the national level across the entire region. Figure 4 shows that governments created a higher number of national-level democratic innovations in the years the left was in office. Brazil, Ecuador, El Salvador, and Uruguay are good examples of intense democratic innovation at the national level during left governments. Honduras, Peru, and Mexico, on the other hand, are exceptions to this rule and proof that the left does not have a monopoly on democratic innovation.

The rise of the left was also closely connected to the increase of deliberative innovations, that is, democratic innovations that rely on deliberation as a primary means of participation. As some left parties were born out of grass-roots movements, they devised more deliberative channels of communication between the state and civil society. In fact, left-leaning parties were behind 60 percent of deliberative innovations created between 2008 and 2015. Left parties may not have a monopoly on participation, but they are strong promoters of deliberation.

The end of the left turn was followed by a sharp decline in democratic innovations. While in 2015 a total of 323 democratic innovations were launched in Latin America, in 2019 this number decreased by 56 percent. The end of the left turn also coincided with a strong decline in deliberative innovations. While in 2015 altogether 110 deliberative innovations were created in the region, in 2019 this number got reduced by 58 percent. Moreover, the role of governments in democratic innovation has drastically decreased across the region in recent years. While in 2015 governments were involved in the creation of 191 new designs for citizen participation, in 2017 this number dropped to 85, a decrease of 55 percent.

As displayed in Figure 5, state-led innovations grew steadily from the 1990s pushed by democratization, constitutionalization, and decentralization efforts, rose quickly during the left turn's peak between 2010 and 2015, and sank drastically after 2016 when the left retreated. In contrast, democratic innovations initiated by civil society have increased considerably since 2010. While the number of state-led innovations created in 2020 was similar to what it was a decade earlier, the number of innovations promoted without the involvement of governments was in 2020 more than double that of 2010.

The rise of authoritarianism in four out of eighteen countries partly explains the decrease of state-led citizen participation in the region and the increase of democratic innovations created by civil society. Since Nicaragua and Venezuela took an authoritarian path, their national governments have implemented almost no innovations. With just a couple of exceptions, since Daniel Ortega reassumed

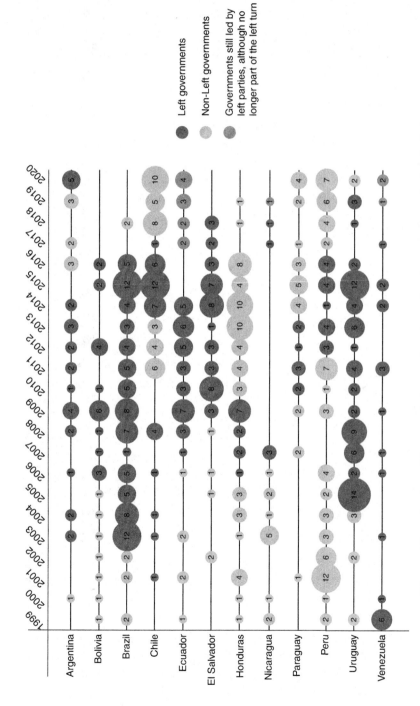

Figure 4 Introduction of democratic innovations by national governments during the left turn

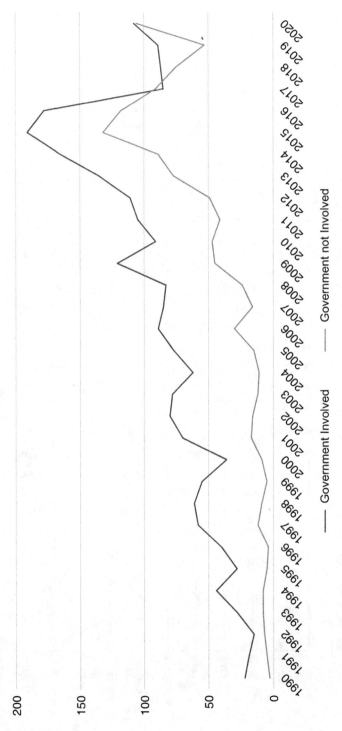

Figure 5 Democratic innovations created per year with and without government involvement

Government Involved — Government not Involved

office in 2007, democratic innovations in Nicaragua have been driven by CSOs, in several cases supported by international organizations. In Venezuela's "competitive participatory authoritarianism" (Mainwaring, 2012), after Hugo Chávez in the early years of his government created some widespread participatory designs such as the communal councils (besides referenda aimed at expanding his power), most state-led democratic innovations have been implemented by local governments facilitated by national legislation promoting participation. Since 2010, only twenty out of fifty-eight democratic innovations implemented in Venezuela have been promoted by the national government. In contrast, civil society implemented thirty innovations without state involvement in the same period.

In El Salvador, since Nayib Bukele took office in 2019, CSOs have been responsible for all four innovations implemented in the country. In Brazil, civil society has been involved in twenty-nine out of thirty-one democratic innovations implemented since Bolsonaro took office in 2019 and dismantled the country's previous participatory institutional architecture. CSO-led innovations in authoritarian countries mostly seek to demand accountability by monitoring government, include historically marginalized groups who are discriminated, and ensure access to social goods and services (especially during the COVID-19 pandemic). Despite all the restrictions to civic space in countries governed by authoritarian presidents, civil society has been thriving and driving democratic innovation.

Digitalization is a major force behind the rise of democratic innovations implemented by civil society, and the fifth aspect that created a favorable context for experimentation with citizen participation in Latin America. The rising curve of democratic innovations implemented without government involvement displayed in Figure 5 is very similar to the rising curve of digital engagement displayed in Figure 6.[5] As shown in the latter, the number of digital innovations (i.e., those that rely on digital engagement as a primary means of participation) created in the region in 2015 was four times higher than just three years before. After a drop between 2017 and 2018, digital democratic innovations created in 2020 were 97 percent higher than in 2019, a boost driven by civil society responses to the COVID-19 pandemic.

Digital engagement has quickly become the main means of participation in Latin America, as it has been used in 55 percent of democratic innovations created since 2016. Except for Central America, where the digital divide is greater and internet penetration lower, in most countries of the region about half of democratic innovations created since 2016 have relied primarily on digital engagement. In Brazil, this proportion is as high as 76 percent. In Mexico, out of

---

[5] The graph shows the number of democratic innovations created per year according to their primary means of participation.

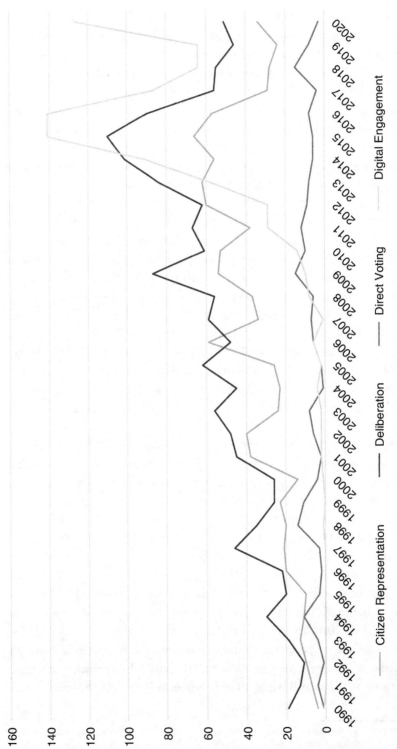

Figure 6 Evolution of means of participation across time

the 329 democratic innovations created over the thirty years, as many as 200 have been implemented since 2012, 54 percent of which rely on digital engagement.

As digitalization expands, civil society organizations innovate more, and the state ceases to be the main promoter of citizen participation in Latin America. However, each country has its own political and social context, which is decisive for democratic innovation, as I have demonstrated elsewhere (Pogrebinschi & Ross, 2019), and which explains the different degrees of influence of all five general aspects that have facilitated democratic innovation in Latin America. Furthermore, specific factors, like party politics and civil society advocacy, also lie behind the implementation of each individual participatory institution, process, or mechanism. The same participatory institution may be adopted for different reasons in different countries (Ganuza & Baiocchi, 2012; Falleti & Riofrancos, 2018; Wampler et al., 2021) or even in different cities within the same country (Wampler & Goldfrank, 2022).

3 Innovations for Democracy

As democratic experimentation has expanded throughout Latin America, a large body of scholarship has dealt with the relationship between citizen participation and institutional innovation in the region (Selee & Peruzzotti, 2009; Cameron et al., 2012; Avritzer, 2017). The heightened role of citizens in policy processes has caught the attention of scholars and has triggered the creation of a new subfield under the label "democratic innovations" (Elstub & Escobar, 2019). The term "democratic innovations" might itself be rather unclear and problematic (Smith, 2019), but it has certainly allowed the literature to converge around a meaning for what has been referred to variously as participatory institutions, participatory innovations, institutional innovations, and institutions of participatory governance or of participatory democracy, among others.

The term "innovation" rightfully captures the sense of experimentation connoted by the new forms of citizen participation it attempts to describe. Likewise, it indicates the underlying suggestion that those "new institutional designs" point to a different notion of democracy. It is mostly this difference, which does not necessarily indicate newness, that renders the term "innovation" appropriate. Democratic innovations comprise forms of citizen participation different than voting, associations, or demonstrations; hence, they innovate vis-à-vis electoral, pluralist, and contestatory forms of citizen participation. In this regard, democratic innovations imply "a departure from the traditional institutional architecture that we normally attribute to advanced industrial democracies" (Smith, 2009: 1).

Notwithstanding, democratic innovations evolve within existing representative democracies. Consequently, these forms of citizen participation are innovative because they are not the default.

While agreeing that "democratic innovations" is a useful term, I believe that the *meaning* it has acquired in the scholarship is misleading because it leaves aside a great deal of empirical evidence from Latin America. In this section, I argue that the current, mainstream concept of democratic innovations contains four problems. The first problem is the assumption that citizen participation is an end in itself, and hence that democratic innovations are designed specifically to enhance it. Instead, I argue that citizen participation is a means to achieve an end, namely the enhancement of democracy. Second, it is assumed that democratic innovations comprise only institutions. Against this, I argue that there are three kinds of democratic innovations, namely, institutions, processes, and mechanisms. Third, the scope of democratic innovations is typically reduced to state-sanctioned institutions. I claim rather that civil society and international organizations are also promoters of democratic innovations. Fourth, there is an expectation that democratic innovations enable citizens to participate in decision-making. Alternatively, I claim that there are four moments of innovation and that citizen participation can take place in all four stages of the policy cycle.

Based on those four points, I propose a more precise and empirically grounded definition of democratic innovations as *institutions, processes, and mechanisms whose end is to enhance democracy by means of citizen participation in at least one stage of the policy cycle.* Unfolding the many parts of this concept will allow me to unpack the analytical framework of this Element and clarify how the problem-driven nature of democratic innovations combines means of participation with democratic ends.

3.1 Participation as a Means of Innovation

Concerns with institutional design have been at the center of debates on democratic innovations. The idea that institutions can be designed to enhance citizen participation has proved attractive to both scholars and practitioners. Such an idea owes a great deal to the widespread definition of democratic innovations as "institutions that have been specifically designed to increase and deepen citizen participation in the political decision-making process" (Smith, 2009: 1). While this definition and other essential contributions to the debate on institutional design were initially based on participatory budgeting in Brazil, the resulting, mainstream notion of democratic innovations does not reflect the evidence regarding Latin America's overall experimentation with citizen participation.

The first and main problem with the concept of democratic innovations is its underlying assumption that participation is an end in itself – and, as such, something democratic per se. This assumption prevails in definitions of democratic innovations as "institutional innovations aimed at fostering citizen participation" (Warren & Pearse, 2008: 3), "reimagining and deepening the role of citizens in governance processes" (Elstub & Escobar, 2019: 22), or, more bluntly, "designed to promote participation" (Avritzer, 2009: 8). While citizen participation is undoubtedly at the core of the concept, the assumption that innovations have been undertaken specifically to increase it fails to reflect their actual democratic meaning.

To begin with, innovations should not be deemed democratic simply because they involve citizen participation. While in principle citizen participation is good for democracy, in practice it is not necessarily democratic. In Venezuela, for example, there is ample evidence that participation in communal councils (widespread local bodies that engage citizens in the formulation and implementation of policy projects) took the form of partisanship (Hawkins, 2010), cooptation, and clientelism (García-Guadilla, 2008). Some studies argue that it was precisely the institutional design of these councils that led to undemocratic participation (López Maya, 2011). Critics seem to agree that the councils undermined participation by causing the involution of civil society and by suppressing the autonomy of social movements (Balderacchi, 2015).

I contend that democratic innovations are democratic because they seek to enhance democracy (1) by addressing its problems, (2) through citizen participation. Citizen participation is, again, not the end but rather a *means* of innovation; hence, citizen participation can take different forms. As I show in the next section, deliberation, digital engagement, citizen representation, and direct voting are the most typical means of citizen participation in democratic innovations developed in Latin America.

Yet democratic innovations may have several ends, one of which may be political inclusion. In those cases, the primary problem to be addressed by the innovation concerns precisely the inclusion of citizens in policy processes. Some innovations may target the inclusion of specific social strata (e.g., those with lower incomes or less education) or underrepresented groups (e.g., women or Indigenous peoples). Under those circumstances, which I explain later in this Element, one can assume an innovation to have been designed to enhance citizen participation. In other words, institutional innovations purposely introduced to increase citizen participation are but one type of democratic innovation, namely, those that aim for political inclusion.

In Latin America, very few democratic innovations would conform to the notion of "minipublics" (Fung, 2003), whose institutional design features can be manipulated in order to promote deliberation and increase participation. Democratic innovations in the region may result from bottom-up pressures from civil society (Ganuza & Baiocchi, 2012) or pro-participation policy entrepreneurs (Mayka, 2019), but only rarely have they been designed for the single purpose of increasing participation. Instead, they are usually created to address specific problems (e.g., the formulation and implementation of health policies) related to broader challenges (e.g., the deficient and unequal provision of a primary social good such as health) and employ citizen participation as a means to achieve a democratic end (e.g., the promotion of social equality).

As Cameron et al. (2012: 13) recognized, "it is not sufficient for citizens to 'come together' ... rather, these institutions need to structure participation and encourage discussions that enable citizens to accomplish a certain purpose." Such purposes are what I call the *ends* of democratic innovation and, based on the LATINNO data, what I claim to be the promotion of accountability, responsiveness, rule of law, social equality, and political inclusion. Innovation for citizen participation is meaningful only when citizens are tasked with advancing one of those "democratic qualities" (Morlino, 2011) and thus stand as "an effective means to accomplish the values of good governance" (Fung, 2015: 514).

Democratic innovations are therefore better understood as a "new practice or process consciously and purposively introduced with the aim of improving the quality of democracy" (Geissel, 2012: 164), except that they are not necessarily new and not always consciously or purposively introduced. In Latin America, many democratic innovations have been introduced or adopted with very little planning and purpose, and their advocates were often not entirely conscious of their future consequences. In countries like Mexico (Zaremberg et al., 2017) and Peru (McNulty, 2019), where democratic innovations have been made mandatory through comprehensive legislation, neither has citizen participation necessarily increased, nor has democracy improved. This reveals an important feature of Latin America's democratic experimentalism: that revisability and fallibility are essential parts of institution-building in the region.

3.2 Three Kinds of Democratic Innovations

A second problem with the prevailing concept of democratic innovations is the assumption that they comprise only institutions. Smith's (2009) pioneering book focused on institutionalized forms of citizen participation and therefore defined democratic innovations as institutions. More recently, he has proposed the use of "participatory democratic institutions" as an organizing concept in place of democratic innovations (Smith, 2019). While now acknowledging that institutions can be more or less formal, Smith maintains the notion, embraced by most democratic innovation scholars, that democratic innovations for citizen participation relate only to institutions.

Such an understanding also persists in the international debate on Latin America's democratic innovations. In his work on participatory budgeting and health councils in Brazil, Avritzer (2009: 4) pushed the term "participatory institutions," defined as being "designed to promote participation." Cameron et al. (2012) also reinforced the institutionalized dimension of a diverse array of democratic innovations across Latin America, which they termed "institutions for participatory democracy" and defined as new forms of "institutionalized voice." In their research on prior consultation in Bolivia and Ecuador, Falleti and Riofrancos (2018: 87) acknowledged the term "democratic innovations" to mean participatory institutions, defined as "formal, state-sanctioned institutions explicitly created to augment citizen involvement in decision making over public goods or social services."

I believe that the diversity of democratic innovations across Latin America clearly indicates that they are not necessarily formal and are neither exclusively state-sanctioned nor only institutions. The more common, restricted understanding derives from the fact that the specialized literature has so far mostly focused on case studies of a few democratic innovations that happen to be proper examples of institutions (and therefore formal and state-sanctioned) – thus the need for more large-N comparative research that can attest to the great variety of forms and shapes of democratic innovations in Latin America. Relying on the LATINNO dataset, I claim that there are three kinds of democratic innovations, namely, institutions, processes, and mechanisms.

3.2.1 Institutions

Institutions fit the established definition of "rules and procedures (both formal and informal) that structure social interaction by constraining and enabling actors' behavior" (Helmke & Levitsky, 2004: 727). Importantly, democratic innovations of the institution kind may be formal and/or informal. In other words, they may also include "socially shared rules, usually unwritten, that are created, communicated, and enforced outside of officially sanctioned channels" (Helmke & Levitsky, 2004: 727). Neighborhood assemblies (*asambleas barriales*) in Argentina are a classic example of an informal participatory institution. On the edge of the country's 2001 economic crisis, citizens began to gather in public spaces, declaring themselves assemblies. These informal institutions consisted of regular open meetings of up to 300 citizens to discuss local problems and voice needs. Hundreds of assemblies quickly spread across Argentina, only demobilizing in 2003.

The quintessential participatory institution in Latin America is perhaps the policy council, which is certainly the most frequent and widespread democratic innovation in the region. Often mandated by law, policy councils have been adopted in all countries at the local, regional, or national level since they were introduced in the early 1990s. They tend to be located within the executive branch, where they provide citizens and CSOs with the opportunity to work alongside policymakers and administrators in charge of drafting, managing, and monitoring public policies. Countries like Argentina, Brazil, and Guatemala have thousands of policy councils at the local level, where they play an important role in the management of social and development policies. At the national level, policy councils have been crucial to policymaking as well as reforms in key areas such as health (Mayka, 2019). Nonetheless, those same participatory institutions have been criticized for being merely "invited spaces" (Cornwall & Coelho, 2007) or subject to cooptation by government and political parties (Balderacchi, 2015).

Just like any institution, democratic innovations may suffer from institutional weakness, facing low enforcement and overall instability (Levitsky & Murillo, 2009). This applies to several formal, state-sanctioned participatory institutions across Latin America, such as regional and local councils in Colombia (Velásquez, 2011), consultative councils in Mexico (Hevia & Isunza Vera, 2012), and the Plurinational and Intercultural Conference on Food Sovereignty in Ecuador (Fiorini, 2015). In these cases, high formalization has not been translated into institutional strength, mostly due to low enforcement. Some of these participatory institutions can be said to have been "born weak," meaning that their creators lacked interest in or the capacity for enforcing them (Levitsky & Murillo, 2009: 120).

3.2.2 Processes

The second kind of democratic innovation comprises *processes* that structure citizen participation across space and/or time toward an end. Processes are composed of at least two instances of participation that may take place simultaneously (in different places) and/or sequentially (in different moments), provided that they are interconnected by the same goal. Furthermore, processes follow procedures involving interrelated steps that participants and policymakers are expected to observe, but unlike institutions they do not constitute regularized practices with a "rule-like quality" (Hall & Thelen, 2009). Participatory processes are organized or enabled by institutions and are usually carried out within them.

As processes, democratic innovations reflect varied institutional designs for citizen participation. Processes often operate as systems in which several parts are interconnected to form a whole (Mansbridge et al., 2012), encompassing both the distribution of work among different spaces and actors (Parkinson, 2012) and the broader relationship between participatory practices and the institutions in charge of taking and implementing political decisions (Hendriks, 2016). While processes can be considered parts of broader participatory and deliberative systems, the concept of a process offers epistemic and empirical advantages. First, it accounts for single, distinct participatory practices structured across space *and* time and interconnected by a shared democratic goal. Second, it characterizes a growing number of hybrid democratic innovations, which combine more than one means of participation or online and face-to-face stages. Third, it accounts for numerous democratic innovations that do not match the "rule-like quality" requirement for institutions, regardless of whether they are state-sanctioned or formalized.

Processes make up 27 percent of democratic innovations in Latin America. They have been customarily employed by governments for the sake of long-term policy planning, in other words, for drafting new policies and setting future strategies and actions alongside citizens and CSOs. One example is the Youth Action Plan, a deliberative process that took place in Uruguay between 2013 and 2014. The process sought to develop strategic guidelines for youth policies and was carried out in three stages. First, twelve "initial dialogues" to identify relevant topics for youth were held, gathering together young representatives from CSOs and political parties who were tasked with formulating proposals. The second stage, the "territorial dialogues," comprised thirty-two workshops held throughout the country and open to people between fourteen and twenty-nine years old. Finally, the third and final stage was the "national youth conference," which gathered in Montevideo over 1,400 young people from all over the country who had participated in the first two stages. The process resulted in Uruguay's second Youth Action Plan, comprising long-term youth policies for the period 2015–2025.

3.2.3 Mechanisms

Finally, *mechanisms* are delimited participatory events intended to address very specific issues. Such democratic innovations are dismantled as soon as their designated aims have been achieved. Unlike processes, participatory mechanisms are essentially single events, which do not unfold across space or time. Yet, combinations and sequences of mechanisms that operate similarly may originate a process (McAdam et al., 2001: 27). Organized or enabled by institutions, mechanisms are sometimes formalized and state-sanctioned, though they tend to be irregular. Mechanisms operate as tools to address concrete problems, instruments to solve specific conflicts, or devices to take particular decisions. Usually short-lived, mechanisms often deal with straightforward issues related to the present moment or to an urgent need or situation. In this sense, they also differ from processes, which tend to deal with future-oriented issues and broader policies.

Almost 40 percent of democratic innovations in Latin America are mechanisms. Typical participatory mechanisms in the region include plebiscites, referendums, popular recall, and popular consultations. These democratic innovations are normally inscribed in law and quite institutionalized. However, regardless of their "rule-like quality" (Hall & Thelen, 2009), once they are implemented their modus operandi is that of a mechanism. All of them consist of single, brief events of direct voting during which citizens participate simply by going to a ballot box and choosing from among two alternatives. Participation in mechanisms is neither regular, as in an institution, nor sequential, as in a process.

A great number of digital democratic innovations are considered mechanisms. For instance, digital campaigns such as mapathons and hackathons are participatory events during which citizens collaborate to identify problems, gather information, assess risks, and search for solutions over a limited time (usually a few hours or days). One example was the Mapathon for Guapi in Colombia, when citizens crowdsourced geographic data that helped control an outbreak of malaria in the city in 2016.

3.3 Innovation beyond the State

The specialized literature has routinely reduced the scope of democratic innovations not only to institutions but even more specifically to state-sanctioned ones. The role of the state in the expansion of new forms of citizen participation has been somewhat overstated by comparative politics scholars and democratic theorists alike. In particular, the literature has, with few exceptions, contributed to the misleading idea that new forms of citizen participation in Latin America are inherently state-driven and thus top-down. Although there may be some truth to that statement, the role of civil society in democratic innovations should not be underestimated. Likewise, the impact of the presence of international funding agencies in the region should not be ignored.

While most countries in Latin America would in one way or another fit Warren's description of "governance-driven democratization," democratic innovations in the region do not belong exclusively to "the domain of non-electoral institutions of government" (Warren, 2009: 5). Furthermore, contrary to the claims of Rich, Mayka, and Montero (2019: 5), participatory institutions are not simply the result of the expansion of state responsibilities or of new policy areas translated into opportunities created by and in the executive for activists. Such a restrictive understanding overlooks aggregated data on democratic innovations in Latin America, as well as differences across countries. Most importantly, it understates the role of civil society during democratization processes and after democratic consolidation.

Governments (in all levels) have been the single promoter of no more than half of all democratic innovations implemented in Latin America since 1990. The state was not involved at all in almost one-third of democratic innovations, including the 19 percent implemented solely by civil society. It partnered with CSOs, international organizations, or private stakeholders in another 20 percent of cases. While the state does indeed have a key role in democratic innovations, the number of cases without any governmental involvement is significant, just like the number of cases in which the state shared power with other stakeholders.

While the data relativize the assumption that citizen participation in Latin America is state-driven, variation across countries should also be taken into consideration. Countries that have mandated democratic innovations through legislation tend to be those where the state is more likely to take the lead. In Brazil, for example, 56 percent of cases were initiated by the state alone. Moreover, countries that have surfed the pink tide have also enjoyed high rates of state involvement in democratic innovations after leftist governments took office. A total of 79 percent of all innovations implemented in Bolivia, 57 percent in Ecuador, and 96 percent in Venezuela between 1990 and 2020 were introduced during left-leaning governments. On the other hand, in Central America, state involvement in democratic innovations is below the 18-country average. In Guatemala, as little as 22 percent of democratic innovations were introduced by the state alone. In Nicaragua, the state was solely responsible for initiating no more than 41 percent of cases.

The comparatively lesser role of the state in the promotion of democratic innovations in Central America can be explained by the strong presence of international development organizations. The latter have been directly involved in one out of every four democratic innovations implemented since 1990 in Central America. In Guatemala, international organizations have partnered with the government in almost as many democratic innovations as it has promoted on its own. In Nicaragua, by contrast, international organizations have provided enormous support to local CSOs for the implementation of democratic innovations, while aiding the government in only few cases.

The role of international development organizations in the promotion of democratic innovations is a highly controversial topic. Whether participation is indeed open and not "induced" is disputable (Heller & Rao, 2015: 3). Scholars suggest that often citizens do not make their voices heard and are turned into service providers who merely supply information (Dagnino, 2010). With similar critiques having been aimed at participatory institutions initiated solely by the state, it remains arguable whether citizens are in general empowered enough to determine the outcomes of democratic innovations (Baiocchi & Ganuza, 2017: 50).

In countries where citizen participation has been state-driven, it has not necessarily been top-down. Brazil, for instance, is the Latin American country with the highest number of state-sanctioned participatory institutions, yet the specialized literature agrees that their design "emerges as a result of different proposals made by social, political, and institutional actors at different moments" (Avritzer, 2002: 150). Brazil's civil society, which was very dynamic during democratization, was actively involved in the draft of the 1988 Constitution as well as in the institutionalization of state-led democratic innovations. The focus of CSOs at that moment was clearly "to establish state institutions that allow for direct citizen participation" (Wampler, 2007: 272).

While state-driven democratic innovation in Brazil has not resulted in top-down participatory institutions, state-promoted citizen participation in Chile has neither really embraced civil society nor resulted in strong participatory institutions. Although Chilean social movements played a crucial role in their country's transition to democracy, they became largely demobilized after consolidation (von Bülow & Donoso, 2017: 15). Chile has developed a stable form of party-based political representation in which professional politicians and a technocratic consensus around the neoliberal model left little room for social movements (Roberts, 1998, 2016). In the two decades following the end of military rule, attempts by Concertación governments to enact policies creating institutional channels for citizen participation only contributed to sweeping civil society aside (Collado, 2018). This critique is extended to Bachelet's first government (2006–2010), whose "citizenship agenda" failed to include civil society and resulted in merely "informative, consultative, and instrumental" participatory institutions (Paredes, 2011). This scenario changed in the context of the 2019–2020 social uprising in Chile, when civil society regained a central role and implemented several democratic innovations alongside the plebiscite that resulted from the protests.

Democratic innovations are thus implemented or comanaged by different political and social actors. They can also be endorsed by very different political projects, which may in turn assign the state and civil society quite different roles in the promotion of citizen participation (Dagnino et al., 2008). Many democratic innovations try to constitute a socio-state interface, a liminal space between the state and civil society that is distinct from both (Elstub & Escobar, 2019) or "hybrids between participation and representation, as well as between civil society and state actors" (Avritzer, 2009: 9). Whether those are "invited" or "claimed" spaces of participation (Cornwall & Coelho, 2007) is a question losing relevance as digital technology blurs those boundaries, empowers civil society, and rapidly changes the political landscape.

3.4 Four Moments of Innovation

The fourth problem with the current concept of democratic innovation is the assumption that it seeks to increase citizen participation "in the political decision-making process." Although it may be desirable that democratic innovations take political decisions themselves, this is not often the case.

In Latin America, about one-third of democratic innovations (34 percent) include citizens in the stage of the policy cycle in which decisions are made, that is the so-called policy formulation stage. Other 2,371 democratic innovations involve citizens in the policy process without entitling them to a role in deciding on the final policy. Citizen participation may precede or follow the decision-making stage, and nonetheless impact policies and improve democracy.

Previous research has shown that citizen participation involves consultation, planning, monitoring, and execution (Falleti & Cunial, 2018: 5–6). Relying on public policy's models of policy cycle (Jann & Wegrich, 2007), I argue that democratic innovations may increase citizen participation in all four stages of the policy cycle, namely, agenda-setting, policy formulation, implementation, and evaluation. This framework seeks to facilitate further assessments of the impact of democratic innovations.

3.4.1 Agenda-Setting

The initial stage of the policy cycle comprises the identification and definition of problems that require political decisions. Citizen participation is crucial at this stage, when problems are recognized as such and the experience of those affected may shape the alternative solutions to be sought by policymakers. Citizens and CSOs participate in dynamics through which ideas, concerns, preferences, and demands are articulated. In 64 percent of democratic innovations, deliberation is the primary means of participation when it comes to defining policy problems and bringing them onto the agenda.

The role of citizen participation in this stage of the policy cycle sheds light on the problem-driven nature of democratic innovations. The democratic innovations enable citizens and CSOs to frame problems and propose solutions, selecting issues that need to be addressed and prioritizing those that should shape the agenda. The process of defining problems and selecting issues includes identifying possible and desirable solutions, and this is how it *sets* the agenda. Innovation happens since citizens and CSOs – and not only experts, bureaucrats, interest groups, lobbyists, and policymakers – define *what* problems should be addressed and provide input on *how* they should be addressed. While they decide on priorities, citizens set the stage for political decision-making later on.

Some democratic innovations involve a more bottom-up approach to agenda-setting, with citizens and CSOs voicing a problem and trying to draw attention to certain issues, as well as public support to demand action from decision-makers. Such cases are successful when citizens and CSOs turn a social problem into a political problem, shaping the policy agenda. One example is Mexico's citizen initiative Law 3of3, which started as a digital platform created by CSOs to foster transparency and evolved into a citizen's initiative calling on public servants to disclose their assets, interests, and tax payments, in addition to other measures to fight corruption. The citizen's initiative gathered 634,143 signatures and ended up being included in an anti-corruption law enacted in 2016. Other democratic innovations involve a more top-down approach, usually when the government aims to address a specific problem and includes citizens and CSOs in the selection of priorities and the proposal of solutions. A good example is Bolivia's first National Dialogue, which in 1997 brought together hundreds of political, social, and economic actors who eventually agreed on a consensus document containing proposals for public policies.

3.4.2 Policy Formulation

The second stage of the policy cycle is divided in two interrelated phases: the formulation of a policy and its adoption. In the first, diverse alternatives for policy design are considered and a policy is drafted. In the second, a decision on which alternative to adopt is made, and the policy is enacted. Although a clear separation between policy formulation and decision-making is practically impossible because both processes are empirically connected (Jann & Wegrich, 2007: 48), the role of democratic innovations is more tangible in the first phase.

While a political decision belongs to the competent institutions, the moment preceding its adoption is marked by intense negotiation among multiple actors who compete to have their preferences considered. Citizen participation mostly takes place during this phase, when political decisions are formed, though not yet finally taken. Nevertheless, research shows that input given during policy formulation often shapes policies even more than the final adoption process (Jann & Wegrich, 2007: 49).

Brazil's National Public Policy Conferences offer an example of how citizen participation can impact policy formulation. Citizens act as crucial sources of information for decision-makers, providing them with knowledge on specific policy issues and enhancing the multidimensionality of policymaking (Pogrebinschi & Santos, 2011). Citizen participation also increases legislative congruence, reduces the informational imbalance between the legislative and executive branches, and augments the responsiveness of policies enacted by legislators belonging to both government and opposition (Pogrebinschi & Ventura, 2017b). Also in Brazil, the digital collaborative formulation of the Internet Civil Framework in 2009 showed how democratic innovations lessen the role of lobbyists and powerful interest groups by giving policymakers direct access to strategic actors and policy communities (Abramovay, 2017).

3.4.3 Implementation

After a political decision has been taken, the policy cycle is only halfway done. Policies still need to be executed and enforced. The implementation stage is critical so that policies are not distorted, delayed in execution, or left only partially or not at all implemented. Citizen participation has been employed to ensure that the policy outcomes achieved correspond to those intended, thus avoiding unsuccessful implementation. Of course, successful policy implementation depends on several factors, from the quality of policy design to available resources and administrative capacities. In Latin America, many democratic innovations have evolved to make up for the lack of state capacity in policy implementation.

About 20 percent of democratic innovations in Latin America target the implementation stage of the policy process. A significant number of those cases involve some form of partnership between government and civil society, with a smaller number involving private stakeholders and international organizations. Many of those innovations are local-level councils and commissions, where citizens and CSOs join public administrators to implement policies in areas as critical as health, education, and housing. Citizens share with administrators the task of making decisions concerning policy implementation, for example, the choice of instruments, selection of strategies, or allocation of resources.

Democratic innovations are also relevant in the implementation of complex policies that require specific local knowledge and of policies with an intersectoral character, which demand collaborative efforts from multiple actors. The implementation of policies in areas such as the environment, rural development, and food security has in the past years increasingly benefited from citizen participation. A compelling example is given by the over 5,000 Water Systems Administrative Boards in Honduras, which include citizens in the operation, maintenance, and administration of the drinking water supply and the sanitation system in rural communities and semi-urban areas.

3.4.4 Evaluation

Democratic innovation takes place during the final stage of the policy cycle by enabling citizens and CSOs to assess whether the problems that originated policies are effectively being addressed. Policy evaluation is "essentially about generating information" (Knill & Tosun, 2012: 175), and civil society can provide information that pushes administrators to improve policy or correct deficiencies in implementation. Citizens may not be entitled to take decisions at this stage, but they make great watchdogs when it comes to evaluating the outcomes of political decisions.

Although only 18 percent of democratic innovations in Latin America focus on evaluation, the number of these cases has risen rapidly in recent years. Almost 500 new designs targeting the evaluation stage have been created since 2010 across the 18 countries, most of them at the national level. Rising levels of dissatisfaction with democracy and distrust in political institutions seem to feed both civil society initiatives to appraise policymakers and government attempts to increase democratic legitimacy by creating novel channels for citizens to render public officials accountable.

Democratic innovations have proved crucial for monitoring complex and intersectoral policy areas, such as the environment. InfoAmazonia, a digital platform developed in 2014, enabled citizens from the nine countries of the Amazon basin to crowdsource geo-referenced information and data on deforestation, fires, mining, and other unlawful actions in protected areas and indigenous lands. In Bolivia, Socio-Environmental Monitoring Committees at the national and local levels assess the socioeconomic impact of extractive industries and monitor their activities in indigenous territories. In Colombia and Ecuador, citizen oversight committees are legally mandated at all levels of the state, allowing citizens and CSOs to exercise vigilance over all sorts of authorities in charge of public management activities.

4 The Means of Citizen Participation

In the previous section, I defined democratic innovations as institutions, processes, and mechanisms whose end is to enhance democracy by means of citizen participation in at least one stage of the policy cycle. In this section,

I argue that as a means to enhance democracy, citizen participation in democratic innovations in Latin America takes four different forms: deliberation, citizen representation, digital engagement, and direct voting. While this classification enables one to distinguish between democratic innovations based on their primary means of participation, it also enables a further differentiation among the concrete institutional designs that have been implemented in Latin America since 1990. In this section, I first provide a comparative analysis of the four means of citizen participation that have taken root across Latin America. Second, I introduce a typology of democratic innovations, while further distinguishing each of the four means of participation.

4.1 Means of Participation in Comparative Perspective

Taken together, the 3,744 democratic innovations in the LATINNO dataset reveal four major forms of participation based on how citizens and CSOs are entitled to participate in those institutions, processes, and mechanisms. As shown in Figure 7, deliberation is the primary means of citizen participation in 43 percent of democratic innovations in Latin America, which translates to roughly 1,602 institutional designs. In second place, a nonelectoral form of citizen representation is the primary means of participation in 28 percent of democratic innovations. Following closely, digital engagement, which just started to expand in recent years, quickly became the primary means of participation in almost one-fourth (24 percent) of democratic innovations in the region. Finally, direct voting, which at some point led experts to define some

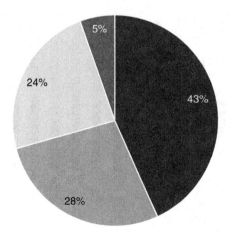

■ Deliberation   ■ Citizen Representation   ▫ Digital Engagement   ■ Direct Voting

Figure 7 Means of citizen participation in Latin America

Latin American democracies as plebiscitarian, is the primary means of participation in as little as 5 percent of the region's democratic innovations.

Deliberation has been largely institutionalized in virtually all countries of Latin America. As I pointed out in Section 2, countries that have taken the left turn are among those that adopted a higher proportion of deliberative innovations. As shown in Figure 8, Argentina, Brazil, and Uruguay, which were governed by the left for long periods, have prioritized deliberation over other means of citizen participation. Left-leaning governments have strongly institutionalized new channels of communication between the state and civil society (Pogrebinschi, 2018). In those countries, deliberation has been an important tool for formulating policies, enabling them to be shaped by the many voices they would likely affect and facilitating agreements between multiple stakeholders, in particular between governments and CSOs. In Central American countries such as Guatemala, Honduras, Nicaragua, and Panama, deliberation is also a favored means of participation. Deliberation has often been used there for agenda-setting, as democratic innovations has enabled citizens to identify problems, define priorities, and propose solutions to be pursued by policies. This focus on "voicing" has been adopted frequently in democratic innovations supported by international development organizations in the context of decentralization processes in Central America. Finally, other countries that have largely relied on deliberation, like Colombia and Costa Rica, have often employed it to harmonize conflicting positions and coordinate among different interests, ensuring that a broader plurality of opinions and demands is considered.

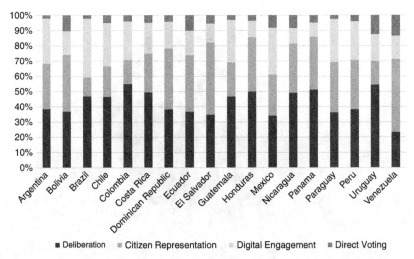

Figure 8 Distribution of means of participation by country

Despite the fact that many thousands of deliberative institutions, processes, and mechanisms have been created across Latin America, the actual deliberative character of democratic innovations has on many occasions remained insufficient. Participatory budgeting offers a good example. In countries like Bolivia, Guatemala, and Nicaragua, national legislation has given participatory budgeting a less deliberative and more consultative character (Goldfrank, 2006). Within Brazil, dissimilar conditions across cities have also affected the deliberative dimension of participatory budgeting, although the decline of such participatory institutions results from factors beyond their inability to promote genuine deliberation (Wampler & Goldfrank, 2022).

Citizen representation is the second most frequent means of participation in democratic innovations in Latin America, although it is frequently combined with deliberation. In fact, almost half of all democratic innovations in the region combine citizen representation and deliberation. This is often the case for management councils and representative councils, participatory institutions seen across most countries of the region. Nonetheless, Venezuela, El Salvador, Dominican Republic, Ecuador, and Bolivia are the countries that have proportionally implemented more democratic innovations relying primarily on citizen representation. In Bolivia and Ecuador, most nonelectoral forms of citizen representation have been adopted to enable underrepresented groups such as Indigenous peoples to participate in representative councils. In El Salvador and Dominican Republic, two countries with high levels of corruption, citizen representation has been mostly used in new institutional designs aimed at citizen oversight, enabling nonelected citizens to monitor elected authorities. In Venezuela, where democratic innovations were often deemed as clientelist and partisan, deliberation not surprisingly was never emphasized, and democratic innovations in which a small number of people act on behalf of many were prioritized.

As of 2020, digital engagement was the third most frequently identified means of participation among democratic innovations, but it will likely soon surpass the others given its rapid rate of growth. Between 2015 and 2020, an average of 104 digital democratic innovations were introduced in the region each year. The three Latin American countries with the highest number of internet users – Brazil, Mexico, and Argentina (Statista, 2021) – are the three countries with the highest number of digital democratic innovations. Likewise, four of the five countries with the lowest number of internet users in the region – Nicaragua, Panama, El Salvador, and Honduras – are precisely those with the lowest number of democratic innovations whose primary means is digital engagement. As internet penetration expands in Latin America in coming years, it is reasonable to expect digital democratic innovations to expand at a similar pace, possibly making digital engagement the main means of participation in the future as I argued in Section 2.

Most post-democratic transition constitutions have included at least one direct voting mechanism such as referenda or plebiscites, and nearly all countries in the region have experimented with them. However, only a few democratic innovations rely on direct voting as their primary means of citizen participation, and they take place less frequently and in fewer countries.[6] Bolivia, Ecuador, Venezuela, Mexico, and Uruguay are the most experienced countries when it comes to direct voting, although the mechanisms preferred in each of these countries varies. Ecuador and Uruguay used to be the countries that implemented a higher number of referendums and plebiscites (Altman, 2011), but after those mechanisms were added to the Mexican Constitution in 2012 and President Manuel López Obrador took office in late 2018, Mexico became the stage for frequent national consultations. Popular consultations have also been implemented to hinder so-called mega projects in countries like Peru, Guatemala, and Colombia. In Colombia, where popular consultations are regulated by the constitution and law, this participatory institution has in recent years been used over a hundred times to challenge large-scale extractive projects (Shenk, 2021). In Bolivia, Ecuador, Peru, and Venezuela, popular recalls are also inscribed in law, empowering citizens to remove elected officials, at both the national and subnational levels, from office.

4.2 A Typology of Democratic Innovations

The four means of citizen participation found in democratic innovations that have evolved in Latin America since 1990 unfold in various designs that can be observed in all eighteen countries. In order to make them measurable and comparable, I developed a typology of democratic innovations. Typologies are crucial for conceptual clarity and comparative research. They help increase analytical differentiation and avoid conceptual stretching (Collier & Levitsky, 2009) and contribute to rigorous concept formation and measurement (Collier et al., 2008). A clear-cut concept based on empirical evidence and a comprehensive typology are essential for making democratic innovations comparable.

Previous attempts to typologize democratic innovations were based on a small number of cases and mostly focused on case studies from the global North. Smith (2009) classified four categories of democratic innovations, namely, popular assemblies, minipublics, direct legislation, and e-democracy.

---

[6] One should also keep in mind that the LATINNO database's methodology, explained in Section 2, prioritizes diversity of designs and does not count each replication of a single democratic innovation, except when its design is substantially changed.

Geissel (2013) relied on a literature survey to distinguish innovations between cooperative governance, deliberative procedures, direct democratic procedures, and e-democracy. More recently, a more robust typology has been offered by Elstub and Escobar (2019), who distinguish among five families of democratic innovations, namely, mini-publics, participatory budgeting, referenda and citizen initiatives, collaborative governance, and digital participation. Those three typologies have two problems. First, they mix means of participation with concrete institutional designs. Second, they rely on a limited set of cases and disregard the vast empirical diversity from Latin America.

In order to improve conceptual description and enable comparability, I have developed a typology of democratic innovations based on a kind hierarchy (Collier et al., 2008; Collier & Levitsky, 2009). A kind hierarchy, just like Sartori's (1970) ladder of abstraction, posits a vertical array of concepts in which subordinate concepts or subtypes are a "kind of" the overarching concept around which the typology is organized. I suggest that democratic innovation, the overarching concept of the typology, is measured by the four means of citizen participation it advances. Therefore, deliberation, citizen representation, digital engagement, and direct voting are the root concepts or dimensions that "capture the salient elements of variation in the concept" (Collier et al., 2008: 223). They are categorical variables that differentiate the categories that appear further down in the typology. These categories, located below each of the four types of democratic innovations, comprise the different institutions, processes, and mechanisms of citizen participation. A participatory institution such as a deliberative council, for example, is a subtype of democratic innovations of the deliberation type. To put it another way, a deliberative council is a kind of deliberative innovation, which in turn is a kind of democratic innovation.

In the typology laid out in Figure 9,[7] the many *subtypes* of democratic innovations (the institutions, processes, and mechanisms structured around the four means of participation) are neither Wittgensteinian conceptual families nor Weberian ideal types but Sartorian "data containers." As data containers (Sartori, 2009 [1975]), they are refined empirical facts that have been quantitatively and qualitatively defined and categorized, drawing on 3,744 cases in the LATINNO dataset. The subtypes of democratic innovations are thus structured around their primary means of participation and qualified by additional properties that allow specification and analytical differentiation.

Although the subtypes are kinds of each of the four types of democratic innovations, it is important to note that in practice, many institutions, processes,

---

[7] In parenthesis is the number of democratic innovations with unique designs that fit each type and subtype, regardless of the number of times and places they were replicated.

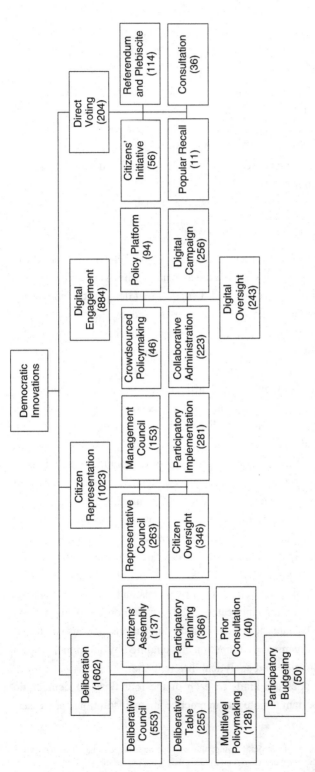

Figure 9 Typology of democratic innovations in Latin America

and mechanisms combine at least two different means of citizen participation. In fact, 59 percent of all democratic innovations implemented in Latin America since 1990 have combined at least two means of participation. For this reason, the typology considers primary as well as secondary means of citizen participation among the defining attributes that allow analytical differentiation. As mentioned earlier, most subtypes of democratic innovations with deliberation as primary means combine with citizen representation as secondary means, and the other way around. Several subtypes of digital innovations often combine with deliberation (policy platforms) or citizen representation (digital oversight) as a secondary means of participation. And occasionally innovations that primarily rely on direct voting are coupled with deliberation (consultations) or citizen representation (citizens' initiatives). The combination of different means of participation in one single democratic innovation is a phenomenon the specialized scholarship has recently recognized and labeled hybridization (Elstub & Escobar, 2019). In the next pages, I introduce each of the four means of participation followed by a brief description of the subtypes of democratic innovations structured around them.

4.2.1 Deliberation

Deliberation is arguably one of the most prominent concepts in democratic theory in recent decades (Dryzek, 2007). It is also possibly one of its most normative concepts. Initially grounded in the notion of legitimacy, deliberation was conceived in procedural terms as aiming to ensure that reasoning and justification among free and equal citizens would yield decisions oriented to the common good, which could be consensually agreed on by those who were then simultaneously their authors and addressees (Habermas, 1996). As the field of deliberative democracy came of age and began to include empirical studies, along with the feasibility and institutionalization problems they entail (Bohman, 1998), the concept of deliberation made clear its vocation for problem-solving.

The very first wave of case studies already showed how well deliberation is suited to identifying and handling public problems, empowering citizens and deepening democracy (Fung & Wright, 2003). Deliberative theory has become increasingly able to combine normative concerns with an orientation toward empirical experiences and problems. Deliberation has been claimed to enable more legitimate and better-informed decisions, improve civic capacities, promote trust and inclusion, and enhance the justice of public policy and the effectiveness of public action, among other positive outcomes (Fung, 2006; Warren, 2008; Smith, 2009).

While deliberation's normative core and its empirical diversity make it hard to achieve consensus on what the concept does or does not entail, Mansbridge's (2015: 27) minimalist definition seems to make room for some agreement: "mutual communication that involves weighing and reflecting on preferences, values and interests regarding matters of common concern." This minimalist definition allows one to perceive deliberation as a *means* that may serve democracy, and not itself an end of democracy. As pointed out by Pateman (2012), deliberation is just a form of citizen participation, and not the other way around.

In Latin America, democratic innovations relying on deliberation use it mostly as a method of problem-solving and of will formation that serves purposes and enables results different from those of aggregative methods like elections or disruptive strategies like protests. In recent decades, deliberation has pursued objectives as varied as concertation and coordination among different interests and stakeholders, problem identification and handling, generation of understanding around public issues, prioritization of alternatives, collective decision-making, and advising.

Deliberation in democratic innovations is frequently used at both the agenda-setting and policy formulation stages of the policy cycle, while it is rather infrequent in the implementation and evaluation stages. Most deliberative innovations are institutions or processes that are implemented by both local and national governments. As the following descriptions of the seven subtypes of deliberative innovations show, they achieve outcomes as varied as opinion formation, preference transformation, collaborative planning, collective input-giving, and dialogical negotiations and agreements.

Deliberative Council

Deliberative councils are participatory institutions designed to promote concertation and coordination between governments and civil society, and often also with other private stakeholders. They tend to be organized around policy areas and include selected representatives of groups primarily affected by the policy in question, ensuring that diverse interests are taken into consideration. Deliberative councils are mostly created by the government and integrated within its institutions. Deliberation is typically used as a method of will formation preceding decision-making, many times providing a forum for the harmonization of opposing interests. One example is El Salvador's National Council of Education, created in 2015 with the goal of promoting dialogue and cooperation in order to reach national agreements on education policy. The Council enables the participation of a wide variety of actors, from education experts to students' organizations, and already in its first year of operation achieved mutual commitments reflected in the El Salvador Education Plan of 2016, which granted continuing education to more than 30,000 teachers, incorporated more than 45,000 students into schools, and renovated roughly 200 school facilities.

Deliberative Table

Deliberative tables are short-lived participatory institutions created with clearly defined goals and targeting specific groups (e.g., Indigenous peoples or young people) or policies (e.g., environment, energy, or security), restricting participation to representatives of those groups and issues being addressed. There are three subtypes of tables: negotiation tables, dialogue tables, and working tables, all of which seek agreement around certain public issues as well as collaboration in solving common problems. One example is Nicaragua's Youth Concertation Table, created in 2014 in Bluefields. The Table brought together CSOs and officials of the municipal and regional governments with the goal of debating, negotiating, and articulating joint actions aimed at solving problems faced by young people, such as poor access to sexual and reproductive health services, employment, and education.

Participatory Planning

Participatory planning is a process that involves one or more spaces or moments in which participants deliberate on long-term policies or policy plans to which a country, region, or city commits. Governments have been the main initiators, though international organizations have supported many cases. Deliberation is structured around the goal of drafting a new policy (or redrafting an existing one) that takes into consideration inputs from those who are potentially affected by or simply share an interest in it. One example was Costa Rica's 2004 participatory process to devise an environmental agenda for water. Deliberative forums with about 400 participants in three regions of the country agreed on ten main problems in water management and possible solutions. The bill for a new water law that resulted from this process was presented to Costa Rica's Legislative Assembly, but it was not ultimately enacted.

Multilevel Policymaking

Multilevel policymaking concerns participatory processes with at least two stages of deliberation, which can take place simultaneously or consecutively and are connected in order to produce a final output. What distinguishes it from participatory planning is the scaling up of deliberation, typically through administrative levels, based on sequenced layers of participation that lead to a cumulative output. Some processes comprise three stages, scaling up from the local to the regional and then the national level. Others involve two stages and scale-up from the local to the regional level or from the regional to the national level. The aim to include input from citizens at all levels that may be impacted by a policy is especially relevant in countries with high regional diversity. The most common examples are the National Dialogues, agenda-setting processes of sequenced deliberation that have been implemented in Uruguay (National Dialogue for Employment, 2011), Ecuador (National Dialogue on Climate Change, 2013), the Dominican Republic (National Dialogue on HIV and Human Rights, 2013), Honduras (Grand National Dialogue, 2015, mostly around transparency and the fight against corruption), and Guatemala (National Dialogue for Justice Reform, 2016).

Citizens' Assembly

Citizens' assemblies are both formal and informal institutions mostly composed of citizens who gather to publicly discuss specific problems that affect inhabitants of a given territory (e.g., neighborhood or community assemblies), common concerns of certain groups (e.g., youth assemblies), or policy-related issues (e.g., health assemblies). Deliberation is often combined with citizen representation, as self-appointed citizens frequently speak on behalf of others who are likewise affected by the issue at stake. By using deliberation to tackle problems affecting participants and those they represent, citizens' assemblies impact the agenda-setting and evaluation stages of the policy cycle. The first citizen assembly to be institutionalized by law was summoned in 1981 in Peru and gave shape to what became known as open town halls. Those *cabildos abiertos* are regularly summoned by municipal governments to discuss local issues and gather suggestions on how to address public concerns. They are active today in Colombia, Dominican Republic, Ecuador, El Salvador, Honduras, Nicaragua, Peru, Uruguay, and Venezuela.

Unlike citizens' assemblies (and other forms of minipublics such as citizens' juries and consensus conferences) that are now gaining momentum in other parts of the world (OECD, 2020), the Latin American *cabildos* do not rely on random selection and informed facilitated deliberation. Until the end of 2020, less than ten citizens' assemblies grounded in random selection and informed facilitated deliberation took place in Latin America. Cases are concentrated in Brazil (besides Fortaleza's Citizen Assembly in 2019, other four minipublics were implemented in São Paulo between 2018 and 2020), Colombia (Bogotá's Citizens' Assembly and "Council to Home," both in 2020), and Mexico (Chihuahua's Citizens' Assembly against Corruption, 2020).

Prior Consultation

Prior consultations foster dialogue and negotiation between Indigenous peoples and the government, and often also private stakeholders (most notably the extractive industry), for the purpose of arriving at consensus or agreements around actions and decisions that may affect their way of life, territories, or natural resources. Although formally an institution mandated by law (the Convention 169 of the International Labour Organization), their modus operandi is mostly of a deliberative process aimed at mutual understanding, though in many cases the final decision is reached through direct voting, with the Indigenous peoples manifesting their approval or disapproval. Except for Dominican Republic, El Salvador, Panama, and Uruguay, all eighteen countries covered in this Element have ratified the ILO's Convention 169 adopting prior consultations. In Costa Rica, Honduras, Nicaragua, and Peru, the government put forward "pre-consultations" to deliberate together with Indigenous peoples the very drafting of the rules concerning future implementations of prior consultations.

Participatory Budgeting

Participatory budgeting engages citizens and CSOs in the discussion of local projects and priorities, and eventually also in decisions about how much of a public budget will be allocated for their implementation. It may concern the budget of an entire city or of certain neighborhoods and may focus on one or more policy areas (e.g., education or health) or address specific social groups (e.g., women or young people). Regardless of its design, it remains essentially a local-level innovation. Citizens gather in neighborhood or sectoral assemblies to discuss investment priorities and select delegates to advance the deliberation further in additional forums or councils, often together with government officials. Participatory budgeting began as a face-to-face process but has since evolved into online and multichannel (combinations of face-to-face, internet, and text messaging) formats.

4.2.2 Citizen Representation

In recent years, several new concepts have tried to grasp the expanding phenomenon in which nonelected citizens stand for others and speak on their behalf without a formal authorization or mandate. Such forms of nonelectoral representation (Urbinati & Warren, 2008) are not exactly new, since groups have long claimed to represent the interests and demands of others without any official delegation. Nonetheless, the rise and spread of democratic innovations has made it necessary to explain the role of the increasing number of self-authorized or self-appointed "representatives" speaking and doing for others in participatory institutions and processes that function similar to representative bodies.

Democratic innovation scholarship has long acknowledged that "most participatory institutions are, in fact, designed in such a way that some citizens represent others, either directly, or – more often – through claims to represent ... those who are not present in the process" (Warren, 2008: 56). Particularly in Latin America, many democratic innovations "do not constitute channels of direct participation for citizens, but rather examples of (indirect) representation of the interest of groups commonly underrepresented in traditional circuits of political representation" (Zaremberg et al., 2017: 4).

Nonelectoral citizen representation takes place when citizens represent themselves or serve in representative capacities. Citizen representatives are mostly lay citizens who represent other citizens within representative structures (Warren, 2008: 50). They may also be members of CSOs who speak or act for others who are not involved with their organizations. Most of the time, these representatives are self-selected, though they can also be selected from within innovations through some act of authorization, whether in a constitutive stage of a participatory institution or at an early stage of a participatory process.

In Latin America, citizen representation as a means of participation within democratic innovations comprises three diverse forms. In the first, citizens are selected to *speak on behalf of others*; in the second, citizens appoint themselves to *stand for the interests and values of others*; and in the third, citizens *act for others*, doing things in their stead.

Citizens speak on behalf of others most often in state-sanctioned participatory institutions or processes where individual citizens or CSOs have (permanent or temporary) seats or assigned roles in the policy process (frequently in the agenda-setting and policy formulation stages). These citizen representatives tend to be authorized by the institution or from within the process. Their selection can occur in various ways, such as by an invitation from or appointment by the government, an election from among a pool of prequalified candidates, or a direct voting procedure involving members of a given community or other representatives within the democratic innovation itself.

Citizens stand for the interests and values of others typically when they share those interests and values and claim to represent them in the absence of actual political representation. In such cases, citizens (as well as CSOs and their members) are self-selected to stand for specific interests (e.g., environment), values (e.g., racial equality), groups (e.g., minorities), or localities (e.g., neighborhoods). Most often, they lack authorization and claim to be representative regardless of whether they are delegated or mandated to do so. This is the kind of representation most likely to resemble intermediation (Zaremberg et al., 2017) or mediation (Cornwall & Coelho, 2007: 15), where citizens and CSOs see themselves as advocates building a bridge between underrepresented groups and the state.

Citizens act for others most often in democratic innovations designed to impact the implementation and/or evaluation stages of the policy cycle. Citizens perform tasks, undertake activities, and literally use their own hands to implement public policies, for example, by building houses, monitoring forests, or distributing water. This kind of citizen representation can be seen as evolving from Pitkin's (1967) "substantive acting for others" or Arendt's (1970) "acting in concert with others."

Democratic innovations with citizen representation as their primary means of participation many times resemble actual representative bodies in that they reproduce the structure of governmental institutions and replicate some of their procedures (e.g., delegation, mandates, voting, majority rule), as the four subtypes described in the next subsection illustrate.

Representative Council

Representative councils are participatory institutions that aim to represent traditionally underrepresented groups in the policy process. They focus mostly on minority groups, providing a venue for them to voice their demands and preferences directly, under the assumption that their presence will improve their political representation. Most representative councils have been created by governments at the national level, usually within the executive branch. Participation is mainly restricted to representatives selected by the groups themselves. Representative councils take up the issues of, for example, Indigenous peoples (e.g., Indigenous Peoples' Advisory and Participatory Council, Argentina), black people (National Committee against Racism and All Forms of Discrimination, Bolivia), women (e.g., National Gender Council, Uruguay), LGBTT people (e.g., National Council of Anti-discrimination of Lesbians, Gays, Bisexuals, Transvestites and Transsexuals, Brazil), children (e.g., National Council for Children and Adolescents, Costa Rica), young people (e.g., National Youth Council, Panama), people with disabilities (e.g., National Council for the Integration of Persons with Disabilities, Peru), and the elderly (e.g., Elderly Citizens' Council, Chile). Representative councils tend to be most active in the agenda-setting stage of the policy process, when they set priorities for the formulation of policies that address the groups at hand. A smaller number of representative councils work at the evaluation stage, monitoring policies and making sure that the groups they represent are not excluded from governmental actions.

Management Council

Management councils are mostly institutions of policy implementation that entitle citizens and CSO representatives to take decisions concerning, for example, resource management, investment prioritization, local project execution, and administration of service delivery. Typically, management councils are in charge of not only what should be done (i.e., which resources for which priorities) but also how it should be done (i.e., who will implement what and how). Participants tend to be ordinary citizens who are self-appointed or internally selected and who speak and act for others without a formal mandate. Sometimes there are delegation processes within councils, such as when they elect internal commissions or working groups tasked with specific assignments. Management councils play a key role in the implementation of social policies at the local level. Most of them deal with basic goods and services like health, education, and housing. Health councils, for example, exist in many countries, including Argentina, Bolivia, Brazil, Chile, Paraguay, Peru, and Mexico. All 5,570 Brazilian municipalities have health councils made up of representatives of government institutions (25 percent), nongovernmental organizations (25 percent), and citizens (50 percent) who meet monthly to implement health policies and administer the allocation of national resources. In Venezuela, more than 45,000 community councils have engaged around 8 million citizens in the management of all sorts of public goods and services, as well as in the implementation of local infrastructure projects (García-Guadilla, 2008).

Citizen Oversight

Citizen oversight refers to participatory institutions that aim to monitor and track the performance of public policies, public servants, service delivery, and government institutions or resources. They have been mostly created by CSOs, with governments solely responsible for less than one-fourth of all such institutions in the eighteen Latin American countries covered. The most frequent forms of citizen oversight are audits, committees, comptrollers, monitors, and observatories. They play a crucial role during the evaluation stage of the policy cycle by assessing the implementation of policies and their effectiveness, as well as the competence of officials and efficiency of institutions in charge of implementation. Citizen oversight is mainly used at the national level, although some countries count dozens or even hundreds of oversight institutions spread across their territories. Participation in oversight institutions is not always open or direct. Apart from ordinary citizens that may occasionally serve as volunteers or collaborators, mostly by providing information and knowledge, CSO staff are the main actors in these institutions. Citizen oversight institutions realize

Pitkin's (1967: 83) belief that "the function of representative institutions is to supply information." In Colombia, the How Are We Doing Cities Network of monitoring programs, led by CSOs in cities across the country, engages citizens in the generation of reliable and impartial information about local quality of life. A 1994 Colombian law empowered citizens and CSOs to exercise vigilance via citizen oversight committees over administrative, political, judicial, electoral, and legislative authorities. These institutions submit reports and recommendations to the supervised entities and state control agencies.

Participatory Implementation

Participatory implementation concerns processes that directly engage citizens in the implementation of public policies. The majority of participatory implementation processes have been initiated by governments, although there are many CSO-driven initiatives that try to cope with the lack of state capacity in certain areas by taking over the delivery of public goods and services. Oftentimes in cooperation with CSOs and international organizations, governments assign groups of citizens (e.g., parents of school children) or entire communities (i.e., inhabitants of given areas) some form of comanagement of policy implementation. Citizens participate by doing whatever necessary for a policy to take effect, for example, making improvements in their neighborhood, distributing food, or policing their communities. By acting for and with others, citizens represent all of those potentially affected by the policy at hand. School feeding programs are emblematic examples, with countries such as Bolivia, El Salvador, Guatemala, Honduras, Nicaragua, Paraguay, and Peru having reportedly implemented successful cases. In Peru, for example, Qali Warma engages citizens' representatives in coadministering and coevaluating the design and implementation of a nationwide school feeding program. Their participation alongside government representatives has improved control of food quality and distribution of food to schoolchildren (FAO et al., 2013).

4.2.3 Digital Engagement

Digital tools are as diverse as the possibilities to use them to boost citizen participation are. It is therefore important to distinguish between digital-based citizen participation as such and democratic innovations whose primary means of participation are digital-based. The first involves various forms of engagement ranging from e-campaigning, e-petitioning, e-polling, and e-voting to online activism and its counterpart slacktivism, plus the uncountable "tiny acts of participation" (Margetts et al., 2015) enabled by social media. The second, with which I am concerned, includes digital mechanisms and processes whose end it is to enhance democracy by means of citizen participation in at least one stage of the policy cycle. Such digital democratic innovations also have multifarious designs, all of which may, however, be able to affect policies by combining digital participation with the end of improving democracy.

Democratic innovations with digital engagement as a primary means of participation necessarily involve some form of active participation in the policy cycle, such as in the identification of problems, the evaluation of their solutions, the collection of ideas for drafting policies, as well as the provision of information necessary for their successful implementation. E-government initiatives that merely rely on digital technologies to make public institutions more transparent and efficient, regardless of whether citizens are involved, do not qualify as democratic innovations. Likewise, some open government initiatives, which are certainly innovative in bringing citizens closer to policymakers, do not actively engage citizens but rather limit their involvement to consultations.

As digital technology expands, the forms of digital engagement in democratic innovations also expand. Among the most recent are crowdsourcing, crowdmapping, and microtasking. *Crowdsourcing* enables an unlimited number of people, the "crowd," to contribute to problem-solving and decision-making by providing inputs, namely ideas, proposals, data, and information. The use of crowdsourcing in the formulation of policies and laws (crowdlaw) has been associated with the improvement of their quality and legitimacy (Noveck, 2018). *Crowdmapping* comprises the crowdsourcing of geographic data with the aim of building a digital map, which can be crucial for solving complex public problems. *Microtasking* implies dividing a large task into many mini tasks that will be collaboratively undertaken by citizens. These forms of digital engagement enable the generation of *collective intelligence*, that is the collaborative sourcing, gathering, and sharing of knowledge from citizens, which increasingly becomes an essential tool for governments that face complex problems and seek to enhance cooperation with civil society to address them (Pogrebinschi, 2020).

Democratic innovations primarily using digital means of citizen participation routinely involve deliberation as a secondary means. Online deliberation is generally referred to as any kind of online discussion, and more specifically as those following principles of deliberative democracy such as inclusiveness, rationality, reciprocity, and respect (Strandberg & Grönlund, 2018). When hosted online, deliberation requires a setup that enables mutual interaction and possibly also the justification of opinions and proposals, as opposed to merely the isolated voicing of citizens. Well-conceived platforms can foster large-scale democratic deliberation among participants as well as the construction of collective knowledge (Aitamurto & Landemore, 2015).

In Latin America, democratic innovations whose primary means is digital engagement are mostly mechanisms and processes initiated by civil society. Altogether, more than half of digital democratic innovations conceived in the region do not involve government at all. Digital engagement is increasingly frequent at the policy implementation and policy evaluation stages, which is when civil society can monitor government performance. Mechanisms of collaborative administration and processes involving digital campaigns, both intended to engage citizens in policy implementation, account for more than half of digital democratic innovations in Latin America. Digital oversight mechanisms make up almost one-third of this kind of innovation, indicating the strong potential of digital engagement at the evaluation stage through policy monitoring. Although digital engagement is less frequent at the agenda-setting and policy formulation stages, policy platforms and crowdsourced policy-making tend to be rather effective. In more than half of crowdlaw processes in Latin America, a law has been enacted as a result of digital engagement.

Policy Platform

Policy platforms are digital websites or mobile apps through which citizens can discuss general concerns or specific policies with one other, and eventually interact with or receive feedback from public authorities. These platforms may allow open interaction, with citizens presenting demands and/or suggesting ideas regarding all sorts of common issues, or they may be restricted to specific policy issues or public matters on which citizens contribute opinions, ideas, and proposals. Although primarily intended to set the agendas of policymakers and administrators, many also impact the formulation of policies. Some are designed to promote deliberation; others simply aggregate opinions, suggestions, and proposals or merely run opinion polls or consultations. An example that combines digital engagement and deliberation is the DemocracyOS platform, developed by a CSO in Argentina in 2012, which facilitated the online public deliberation of bills of law introduced in the Buenos Aires city legislature in 2015. The platform stimulates better arguments in a discussion forum with predefined discussion rules and was later used by the Mexico's federal government to develop an open government policy.

Crowdsourced Policymaking

Crowdsourced policymaking involves digital platforms where citizens collaboratively participate in the formulation of laws or policies by sketching out ideas, providing content, suggesting modifications, or making substantive comments on new norms (including regulations and constitutions) being proposed to or enacted by elected representatives. These digital processes are generally led by governments (legislative or executive branches), who seek to gather knowledge and information from citizens in order to formulate better and more legitimate laws and policies. A groundbreaking and successful example of crowdlaw is Brazil's Internet Civil Rights Framework, which, between 2009 and 2010, brought government and civil society together in the formulation of a law regulating the governance and use of internet in the country. The participatory process had two stages. The first enabled citizens, CSOs, and private stakeholders to contribute inputs, including substantive comments and alternative draft proposals. The second stage allowed participants to comment directly on a draft of the law. The collaboratively drafted bill of law was sent to the legislature in 2011, where it underwent another round of digital discussion, and was finally enacted as a law in 2014.

Collaborative Administration

Collaborative administration concerns digital collaborative platforms or apps through which citizens can report problems to public administration authorities. Most of them employ geolocation, are implemented at the local level, and deal with urban issues. Many, but not all, collaborative administration mechanisms provide responses from public authorities on how reported problems were addressed. These digital mechanisms of citizen participation are designed to improve the implementation of policies using feedback and information generated by citizens. One example is Bacheando, a digital app that allowed the citizens of Asunción, Paraguay, to report to municipal authorities the presence of potholes on the streets. After citizens submitted geolocated information and sent pictures, they could track the status of the repairs, which were continually updated until completion. In Chile, collaboration between a CSO and government enabled the platform Neighborhoods in Action, which allowed citizens to report to their municipal authorities about all sorts of urban problems and propose solutions to them, in addition to discussing local problems with neighbors.

Digital Campaign

Digital campaigns are mainly events or actions with definite durations and clear goals. The most prevalent forms of these mechanisms are hackathons, mapathons, and online campaigns around the rejection or approval of policies or laws. *Hackathons* are brief events during which participants collaborate to develop solutions for specific public problems as well as to propose ideas and initiatives to improve public life. *Mapathons* are coordinated collaborative mapping and data-generation efforts in which citizens produce or improve maps geolocating and identifying public issues that need to be addressed by the authorities. Other *online campaigns* involve attempts to mobilize citizens around support for or the rejection of bills, laws, policies, or other governmental acts. These include platforms or apps where citizens can send direct messages to elected officials, sign manifests or petitions, or cast online ballots indicating their preferences. An example of a digital campaign was the Gender Violence Map, a collaborative mapping implemented by a CSO in Brazil that sought to make visible the vulnerable situation of women and LGBT+ people, as well as to point out how the lack of data on gender violence hinders public policies. The map comprised data contributed by citizens, governments, and CSOs. Following the mapping, an information campaign that highlighted gaps in data on gender violence was launched, and the CSO collaborated with governmental organizations to fill those gaps.

Digital Oversight

Digital oversight comprises digital platforms and mobile apps focusing on tracking and monitoring public policies, public servants, public service delivery, institutions, or resources. Some allow citizens to report wrongdoings or make complaints, generating public awareness. Others collect and publicize public data for transparency and accountability purposes. Although usually open in nature, digital oversight is sometimes restricted to a group of individuals who do the monitoring and receive information from citizens. Digital oversight mechanisms are usually designed by CSOs to impact the evaluation stage of the policy cycle. One example is the Local Observatories, consisting of four digital platforms developed in Bogota, Colombia, in 2011, which made it possible for citizens from four neighborhoods to monitor the activities and investments of the local administration.

4.2.4 Direct Voting

Though not new, mechanisms of direct democracy are commonly considered democratic innovations (Elstub & Escobar, 2019).[8] Although voting is an indispensable characteristic of most such democratic innovations, citizens do not vote to elect representatives who will decide on their behalf. Rather, they vote directly to decide or express opinions on policy issues or political matters.

---

[8] As mentioned in Section 3, direct voting mechanisms are inscribed in law and quite institutionalized. However, though they are conceived as institutions, their modus operandi is that of a mechanism.

Mechanisms of direct voting are thus not a default form of citizen participation, but, pointing to an altogether different notion of democracy (direct democracy), they depart from the traditional institutional architecture of representative democracy and are in this regard innovative.

Mechanisms of direct voting have existed in Latin America since before the process of constitutional reforms associated with the third wave of democratization. Today, most constitutions ensure that citizens can vote on issues in referendums and plebiscites, propose legislation through popular initiatives, reject extractive industry mega projects via popular consultations, and, where recall is institutionalized, terminate the mandates of elected representatives. Democratic innovations based on direct voting can be mandatory or facultative, binding or consultative, proactive or reactive, top-down or bottom-up (Altman, 2011). When they are mandatory or binding, then citizens do in fact directly take part in the political decision.

Though they serve to expand citizen participation, direct voting mechanisms and processes are routinely criticized because of very high levels of abstention and social selectivity, which reproduces or even deepens inequalities, either because less-educated groups lack sufficient access to information or due to outcomes that harm disadvantaged populations and minorities (Merkel, 2011). The evidence from Latin America is inconclusive. Some scholars argue that because representative institutions are unstable and weak, direct voting mechanisms may undermine political parties and party systems (Altman, 2011). Others claim that political parties have always retained centrality despite extensive use of direct voting, and new party identities have even been generated as a result (Lissidini, 2010). Some scholars believe that the region's characteristic (hyper)presidentialism has facilitated the manipulation of direct voting mechanisms by populist presidents (Breuer, 2007), while others counter that direct voting does not necessarily enhance executive power and that presidents are not always able to manipulate them (Durán-Martínez, 2012).

Despite charges of populist and plebiscitarian uses of direct voting in Latin America, especially in the Andean region (Levitsky & Loxton, 2013), such democratic innovations have enabled citizens to decide on a few substantive matters, especially through popular consultations and citizens' initiatives. Most referendums and plebiscites, however, have dealt with questions of institutional design or contingent politics (e.g., extensions of mandates, presidential reelection, or constitutional assemblies), while decisions on substantial matters and specific policy issues were far more rare (Altman, 2011). In the next subsection, I describe briefly each of these institutions that nevertheless operate mostly as participatory mechanisms or processes.

Citizens' Initiative

Citizens' initiatives are processes of collecting signatures from citizens for different purposes. Typical cases involve the drafting of a bill of law (a legislative proposal) and the collection of support for its submission to the legislature (local, regional, or national). Citizens' initiatives increasingly combine direct voting and digital engagement, as a few processes of collecting signatures start to take place online. Many citizens' initiatives are regulated by laws or constitutions, which define how many signatures are needed for citizens to propose initiatives. Not all cases are binding, meaning that the legislature may not consider the initiative. Other citizens' initiatives include the collection of signatures with the aim of opposing legislation (*iniciativa de veto popular* in Colombia) or demanding a consultation, plebiscite, or referendum (*solicitud de referendum* in Uruguay). A well-known example of a citizens' initiative is the "Clean Record" legislative initiative that in 2009 gathered around 1.6 million signatures in Brazil seeking to make ineligible for office politicians who had been convicted, had a mandate revoked, or had resigned to avoid impeachment. The initiative was passed into law in 2010, only a few months after being submitted to the legislature.

Referendum and Plebiscite

Referendums and *plebiscites* are voting mechanisms in which citizens can directly express their preferences regarding a limited set of options. The two terms are used almost interchangeably across Latin America, given that each country's constitution regulates these mechanisms in different ways (Altman, 2011). Mandatory referendums take place on occasions required by constitutions, while facultative referendums result from individual or collective initiatives. The outcomes of these mechanisms are not always binding. A well-known example is the Plebiscite for Peace that took place in Colombia in 2016 with the aim of approving or rejecting the peace agreement that had been negotiated between the Colombian government and the FARC, the largest guerrilla group in the country. The agreement had been negotiated over four years and was expected to end more than fifty years of armed conflict. The final decision was granted to the citizens of Colombia, only 37 percent of which actually voted, and the agreement was rejected by a narrow 0.4 percent. The plebiscite had been preceded by various democratic innovations that sought to debate the terms of the agreement and has shown how extensive deliberative processes can also be overthrown by direct democracy mechanisms.

Popular Recall

Popular recall is a mechanism that allows citizens to prematurely terminate the mandates of elected officials. It originates with a citizens' initiative to remove an elected official and, once a certain threshold for signatures has been met, is usually followed by a referendum. For this reason, popular recalls are also referred to as a "recall referendums." The procedure varies from country to country, though it has actually been adopted in only a few, mainly Andean, countries. In Peru, over 20,000 popular recalls took place at the subnational level by 2017 (Welp, 2018). In Bolivia, a national recall referendum took place in 2008 to decide whether the president and eight of nine state governors would keep their positions. Everyone remained in office, except for two state governors who had their mandates revoked.

Popular Consultation

Popular consultation constitutes a bottom-up mechanism of direct voting in which citizens cast ballots to express support for or opposition to a given question or proposition. Unlike prior consultations (regulated by ILO Convention No. 169), they neither involve deliberation nor seek consensus. Yet even when popular consultations are promoted by governments, their results are often not binding. There are also popular consultations triggered by citizens' initiatives in addition to others more informally promoted by CSOs and addressing a wide range of topics. Also rarely binding, such cases many times still serve to set the agenda and identify solutions to public or local problems. A prominent case was the popular consultation on water that took place in Cochabamba, Bolivia, in 2000, which sought to settle the so-called "water war," a series of bloody protests triggered by the privatization of the local water supply company. More than 50,000 citizens voted against the privatization and demanded its cancellation, which ended up happening despite the consultation's informal and nonbinding nature.

5 The Ends of Democratic Innovations

Means are commonly said to justify ends, but when it comes to democracy, means and ends are equally relevant and depend on each other. Democratic ends demand democratic means for their realization (Dewey, 1939: 175). Deliberation, citizen representation, digital engagement, and direct voting can improve democracy only if they are means for citizens to address problems that hinder it. The institutions, processes, and mechanisms that we call democratic innovations are not designed simply to increase citizen participation but rather to attain democratic ends.

This section will underscore the ends pursued by democratic innovations, namely, accountability, responsiveness, rule of law, social equality, and political inclusion. While these ends have been identified within the empirical cases, they also reflect both evaluative standards conceptualized by democratic theorists and dimensions of the quality of democracy devised by comparativists. I claim that, in their attempt to pursue one or more of these five ends, democratic innovations seek to address problems that can be related to challenges faced by democracy in Latin America, namely, deficits of representation, the (un)rule of law, and inequality. While I do not argue that democratic innovations respond directly to those challenges, I argue that they are able to address – by means of citizen participation – concrete problems that hinder democracy, such as, for example, corruption, lack of transparency, unresponsive policies, absence of public security, gender inequality, or racial discrimination.

This problem-driven approach to democratic innovations, in which means of participation and ends of innovations combine to address public problems, reflects Latin America's democratic experimentalism or what I earlier called pragmatic democracy (Pogrebinschi, 2013; Pogrebinschi, 2018). The first part of this section introduces this pragmatist approach, showing how the five ends combine and reflect dimensions of the quality of democracy. It also presents a brief comparative analysis of the ends pursued by democratic innovations across Latin American countries. The second part of this section describes the features of democratic innovations primarily oriented to each of the five ends, connecting them with the types of problems they seek to address. Finally, this section presents data on impact and discusses the extent to which democratic innovations in Latin America have achieved their ends.

5.1 Combining Means and Ends

While democratic innovations have been long defined as institutional designs aimed to increase citizen participation in decision-making, they are commonly assessed based on the democratic standards they are expected to achieve. Fung, writing of "functional consequences" (2006) and "democratic values" (2015), argues that citizen participation may advance the three major values of legitimacy, justice, and effective governance. Smith (2009) proposes that innovations should be assessed on the basis of how they realize the four "democratic goods" of inclusiveness, popular control, considered judgment and transparency, and the two "practical goods" of efficiency and transferability. Geissel (2012) suggests four dimensions to assess how participatory institutions affect the quality of democracy, namely, input-legitimacy, democratic process, effectiveness, and civic education. Warren (2017) claims that, to count as democratic, practices (including deliberation, representation, and voting) should serve three necessary "functions," namely empowered inclusion, collective agenda and will formation, and collective decision-making. Looking at Latin America,

Cameron et al. (2012) evaluate participatory institutions based on the criteria of inclusion, representation, responsiveness, disruption of clientelism, accountability, and citizens' education.

These standards set important normative horizons for democratic innovations. However, if innovations are expected to improve democracy, they should be able to raise the same standards against which existing democracies are usually measured. Such standards are offered by the scholarship on the quality of democracy. Morlino (2011) proposes eight dimensions or "qualities" to empirically evaluate democracies, namely, participation, competition, responsiveness, electoral accountability, interinstitutional accountability, rule of law, freedom, and equality. These dimensions are also present in indicators used by indexes that measure democracies around the world such as the Varieties of Democracy (V-Dem).

What I define as the *ends* of democratic innovations rely both on these "democratic qualities" and on the concrete cases in the LATINNO dataset, as explained in Section 2. These cases reveal that the problems democratic innovations seek to address, and consequently the areas where they seek to make improvements, relate to four of these "qualities," specifically accountability, responsiveness, rule of law, and equality. Additionally, the data show that democratic innovations in Latin America often deal with matters of political inclusion, such as gender and ethnic discrimination, which Morlino (2011) considers under the equality dimension. I differentiated political inclusion from social equality by creating specific indicators for each, arriving thus at the five ends of innovations.

The five ends reflect thus standard measures of democracy and can be used to assess the impact of citizen participation. Democratic innovations may enhance democracy when they improve at least one of the five ends. Figure 10 displays the pragmatist analytical framework in which means of participation and ends of innovations combine to enhance democracy.

Democratic innovations may combine more than one means with one or more ends, depending on the problems they aim to address. Just to make clear how it works, take the example of Uruguay's National Council on Gender. The law that created it in 2007 says that the council should "integrate the voices from the state, the academy, and civil society" in the "design, execution, and evaluation of public policies that incorporate a gender perspective," in order to promote the "effective recognition of women," besides "overcoming inequalities." As with most representative councils, it combines the means of citizen representation and deliberation. The "voices" to be integrated are those that are represented. While seeking to both promote the recognition of women and reduce inequality, the National Council on Gender combines the ends of political inclusion and

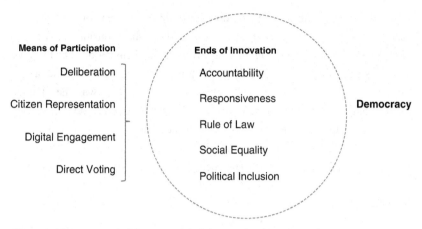

Figure 10 Means of citizen participation and ends of democratic innovation

social equality. This combination of means and ends is the core of democratic experimentalism, a term that embodies a sense of change and improvement, but also of fallibility. The de jure attributes of the Gender Council may de facto end up looking very different, and no actual deliberation may take place nor political inclusion achieved.

In a broader perspective, democratic experimentalism points not only to how means and ends might combine within the same democratic innovation, but also to how, in a more systemic perspective (Mansbridge et al., 2012) or problem-based approach (Warren, 2017), diverse democratic innovations, oftentimes based on different means, interrelate in their pursuit of a single or even multiple ends. Chile has recently offered a fascinating example of how this happens. The plebiscite that in late 2020 decided that a new constitution should be drafted by a national convention was not merely a result of the massive protests that took Chilean streets between 2019 and 2020. Since the very onset of the social outburst (*estallido social*) more than a thousand citizens' assemblies have been self-organized throughout the country, drawing together many thousands of citizens. Those *cabildos ciudadanos* were highly deliberative, and numerous participants were speaking on behalf of others or standing for the interests and values of others, hence representing other citizens without an official mandate. Combining thus deliberation and citizen representation, the citizens' assemblies played a very important role in setting the agenda, not only around the need for a new constitution, but also regarding the demands it should respond to.

Other democratic innovations implemented in Chile between the start of the protests and the plebiscite employed combinations of the four means of participation to pursue greater responsiveness. On the government side, two innovations were implemented under the name "The Chile That We Want." The first was the

"Dialogues" that combined deliberation and citizen representation in citizens' assemblies organized at the local level; the second was the "Consultations" which took place nationwide in a digital platform without deliberation. On the civil society's side, Chile's two main universities jointly implemented two innovations under the name "We Have to Talk About Chile." The first was the "Digital Conversations," which comprised a thousand online citizens' assemblies composed of four to eight people who, selected according to socio-demographic criteria and facilitated by a moderator, deliberated on the country's main problems and proposed solutions to them. The second was a nationwide consultation on a digital platform that asked eighteen questions related to substantive policy issues that could later feed into the new constitution.

Figure 11 shows that responsiveness is the most frequent end sought through citizen participation in Latin America, comprising 33 percent of all democratic innovations, followed by social equality (21 percent), accountability (19 percent), political inclusion (17 percent), and rule of law (10 percent). Figure 12 shows how means and ends combined in Latin America between 1990 and 2020. It considers only the primary means and the primary ends of each innovation. The data provide interesting clues about which means are considered more suitable for addressing which ends. For instance, responsiveness has been most frequently pursued through deliberation, which makes sense given that this is the means of participation that better enables citizens to express their preferences and voice their demands, making it more likely that policies will actually address them. Though to a lesser degree, social equality and political inclusion have also been sought via deliberation, which is explained by the presence of deliberative, management and representative

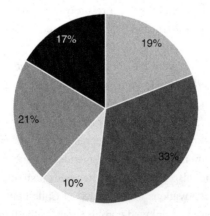

Accountability   Responsiveness   Rule of Law   Social Equality   Political Inclusion

Figure 11 Ends of democratic innovations in Latin America

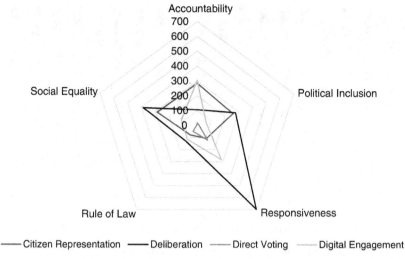

Figure 12 Combinations of means and ends in Latin America

councils all over Latin America. By contrast, perhaps due to their very nature, those two ends have hardly been the object of digital engagement. The latter seems to be more suitable for innovations that target accountability and responsiveness; think of the numerous mechanisms of collaborative administration and digital oversight, as well as processes of digital campaigning.

Despite their smaller number, democratic innovations primarily relying on direct voting provide a straightforward illustration of how ends relate to specific designs. Most citizens' initiatives pursue responsiveness as they aim precisely to have citizens' ideas and preferences identified and addressed. Popular recalls aim at improving accountability as they are clearly designed to render officials accountable by revoking their mandates. Most referendums and plebiscites target responsiveness, as they enable citizens to directly confirm or reject a proposition according to their preferences. The same is true for most popular consultations, but, because of the nature of the issue at stake, many of them are seen to pursue social equality.

Some of the countries with a greater number of democratic innovations aimed at responsiveness, such as Argentina, Chile, Costa Rica, and Colombia, are also among those that contain a higher number of deliberative innovations (as seen in Figure 8). In other countries employing a very high number of deliberative innovations, like Brazil, deliberation has been more often used to achieve social equality. Brazil is in fact home to the highest number of democratic innovations aiming to promote social equality, exactly half of each implemented in the thirteen years that the country was ruled by the leftist Workers' Party (2003–2016).

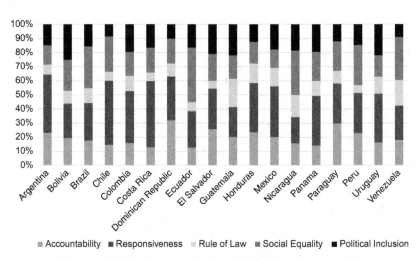

■ Accountability ■ Responsiveness ▦ Rule of Law ■ Social Equality ■ Political Inclusion

Figure 13 Distribution of ends of innovations by country

Along with Brazil, Ecuador, Nicaragua, and Venezuela are the countries with the higher share of innovations aimed at achieving social equality. In these countries, left-leaning governments have clearly embedded citizen participation in their overall strategy to reduce social inequality. But this has not been the case in all countries that turned left. In Uruguay, for example, the left invested comparatively little in democratic innovations aimed at social equality. Uruguay is, however, the least unequal country in Latin America.

Figure 13 gives indications of how ends relate to problems which are more accentuated in some countries. Dominican Republic, Paraguay, and Honduras are countries with a higher share of democratic innovations aimed at increasing accountability; notably they also rank among the top five most corrupt nations in Latin America. Bolivia and Guatemala are countries that have a larger percentage of innovations that seek to increase political inclusion, while almost half of the population identify as Indigenous in both countries. The countries scoring lower on rule of law indicators in the region, namely, Guatemala, Nicaragua, Honduras, and Venezuela, have a higher number of democratic innovations aimed at strengthening rule of law compared to other means, more than half of which is pushed by civil society. Likewise, the countries with the highest rule of law scores in the region, Chile and Costa Rica, have implemented relatively very few such innovations.

Yet, structural problems that affect some countries may not always work as triggers for democratic innovations. Black people account for almost half of the population in Brazil and suffer systemic discrimination; nonetheless, in the country that accounts for the most democratic innovations in the region, only 15 percent of them are aimed at increasing political inclusion. Colombia has been struggling with armed conflict for several decades; despite being the country with the third most democratic innovations in the region, only 11 percent of them address problems related to the rule of law. Although democratic innovations are problem-driven, they are not themselves exempt from problems. And they are often unable to achieve the ends they were purportedly designed to address.

5.2 The Problem-Driven Nature of Democratic Innovations

The widespread deficits of representation in Latin America are often associated with the rise of democratic innovations in the region (Selee and Peruzzotti, 2009). Yet, while the cure for the ills of representative democracy has usually been more broadly understood as the provision of a "greater voice for citizens" (Cameron et al., 2012: 4), I argue that citizens' participation has been adopted mostly as a means to achieve an end, and not as an end itself.

As problem-driven participatory designs, democratic innovations in Latin America aim, above all, to enhance democracy by using citizen participation to tackle concrete problems that may hinder democracy. In this subsection, I rely on empirical evidence taken from the LATINNO dataset to describe the most frequent problems that democratic innovations seek to address and how they relate to the five ends discussed in this subsection.

5.2.1 Accountability

Democratic innovations whose primary end is to achieve accountability comprise nonelectoral forms of rendering governments, political institutions, and elected representatives further answerable for their actions and inactions. While democratic innovations are themselves commonly associated with what is called social accountability, many of them are clearly concerned with improving political accountability.

As summarized in Table 1, three main sets of problems, namely flawed elections, low trust in political parties, and ineffective governance, are the targets of innovations whose primary end is accountability. Democratic innovations that deal with problems related to *flawed elections* seek to bolster electoral accountability, for example, by ensuring clean electoral processes, curbing irregularities during electoral campaigns, augmenting the ability of citizens to make informed choices, avoiding voter suppression, and inhibiting clientelist and personalistic voting. Democratic innovations concerned with *low levels of trust in political parties* seek to strengthen the parties by, for example, increasing their channels of communication with voters, informally vetting candidates, and evaluating the performance of elected representatives. Finally, democratic innovations that

Table 1 Innovations aimed at accountability

Problems	Aims
Flawed elections	Enable oversight of electoral campaigns, polling stations, and vote counting to curb electoral malpractice, bribery, and voter intimidation
	Ensure informed voting; avoid disinformation campaigns; check facts and data
Low trust in political parties	Increase channels of communication between representatives and citizens
	Enable citizens to give input and receive feedback, and monitor performance of representatives
Ineffective governance	Monitor public services and ensure quality of service delivery
	Prevent improper use of public resources; increase transparency and access to public data and information

target problems associated with *ineffective governance* aim to, for example, enhance the effectiveness of public services, prevent the improper use of public resources, ensure transparency, and reduce corruption.

Accountability-oriented democratic innovations share three main characteristics: most of them are implemented by CSOs, employ digital engagement as their primary means of participation, and are used at the evaluation stage of the policy process.

Only 27 percent of the 711 democratic innovations that primarily aim at improving accountability have been implemented by governments alone, likely because political reforms undertaken by the state usually focus on improving existing political accountability institutions instead of innovating with new designs or allowing citizens to assume more control. However, they can be prodded to implement innovations oriented to accountability when they partner with CSOs or international organizations. In fact, during the 1990s and 2000s, in the context of decentralization processes when international development organizations played a significant role in boosting democratic innovation, it was not uncommon for local and national governments to implement innovations aimed at improving accountability. The government of Bolivia, for example, received in 1995 a five-year grant from the United States Agency for International Development, promising to foster accountability, transparency, and administrative efficiency through citizen participation. In the context of the resulting "Democratic Development and Citizen Participation Project," a planning process was designed that included several deliberative stages, in which citizens and groups were expected to participate in the definition of priorities and the drafting of policies, while overseeing their implementation by local governments.

Since the expansion of digital technology after 2010, democratic innovations that seek to enhance accountability have relied mostly on digital engagement, and civil society has become the main promoter of democratic innovations with that end. Close to half of all accountability-oriented democratic innovations rely on digital technology for engaging citizens. Digital tools have expanded possibilities for oversight and diversified forms of citizen monitoring in recent years. Not only have information and data become more accessible, but "watchers" have multiplied and become mobile. Citizen efforts to oversee political institutions, elected representatives, and policy implementation have substantially increased with digital technology. Digital oversight mechanisms should soon supersede citizen oversight institutions as the most frequent type of democratic innovations created to tackle accountability problems in Latin America.

The number of internet platforms and mobile apps developed to oversee electoral processes and curb electoral malpractice across Latin America has quickly increased in recent years. Those digital democratic innovations mostly monitor electoral campaigns, polling stations, and vote counting. They enable citizens to report irregularities during elections in real time using geolocation. In a growing number of cases, this information may be conveyed directly to electoral authorities. One year before Guatemala's 2015 general elections, for example, CSOs developed Eye Guate, an app enabling citizens to report premature campaigning by transmitting information and pictures to the Supreme Electoral Court, which sanctioned eleven parties as a result. In Argentina's 2015 elections, citizens used the app Eye on the Vote to report around 2,500 election-day irregularities, ranging from lack of ballots in polling stations to violent voter intimidation tactics. In Colombia's 2018 national elections, the app Mapee enabled citizens to inform authorities when candidates did not comply with propaganda regulations. Colombia's National Election Council, which codeveloped the app, received around 900 reports of irregularities in electoral campaigns, and used them to monitor compliance and apply sanctions on candidates and parties.

5.2.2 Responsiveness

Democratic innovations aimed at improving responsiveness seek to expand forms of signal emission from citizens regarding their policy preferences, demands, opinions, and needs. They also comprise forms through which these signals can be received by governments in order to be considered in their

Table 2 Innovations aimed at responsiveness

Problems	Aims
Unresponsive policies	Expand opportunities for expression of citizens' preferences and their reach
	Include citizens in agenda-setting and policy formulation
Low levels of trust in legislatures	Increase transparency; improve institutional performance; track legislators' activities
	Enable citizens to send proposals, comment, and discuss ongoing projects

decisions and actions. Behind many of these innovations is a manifest concern with tackling citizens' mistrust of politics, reversing their perceptions of inadequate representation, or simply enhancing the legitimacy of political decisions.

Democratic innovations whose primary end is responsiveness attempt to address two related problems: the unresponsiveness of policies and the low level of trust in legislatures (see Table 2). Democratic innovations concerned with *unresponsive policies* seek to enable citizens to express their preferences further and more clearly, no matter which policy is at stake. Their goal is to give citizens opportunities to have their ideas and opinions taken into consideration by policymakers, trying to ensure that any outcomes will more genuinely reflect their preferences. While participatory innovations per definition aim at increasing the input of citizens in the outcome of policies, those with responsiveness as the primary goal are chiefly concerned with augmenting issue congruence between preferences and policies and strengthening political representation. Democratic innovations that seek to address *low levels of trust in legislatures* try to strengthen the channels of communication between citizens and policymakers, enabling exchange and interaction. They also aim at making legislative activity more visible and transparent by enabling citizens to have some degree of participation in the mandate of their elected representatives, either by setting their agendas or by monitoring their work. Several of those innovations also seek to make legislatures more open, allowing citizens to take part in the formulation of policies.

The 1,209 responsiveness-oriented democratic innovations have three main features. They are mostly implemented by governments both at the local and national levels, have deliberation as their primary means of participation, and are designed to impact the agenda-setting and policy formulation stages.

Deliberation proves to be very suitable for pursuing responsiveness, as it allows for coordination and collaboration during the formulation of policies, in addition to enabling citizens to form and transform their preferences during agenda-setting. Deliberative councils, implemented by governments at both the national and local levels, are the most frequent type of innovations primarily aimed at responsiveness. Yet, participatory planning has likely produced the most impact. The Participatory Strategic Plan of Santa Tecla in El Salvador, for example, was a deliberative process that enabled citizens to propose short-, medium-, and long-term projects to be implemented by the city. In 2002, it brought together some 150 representatives of civil society in 37 roundtables tasked with discussing with public authorities the directions, priorities, and actions to be developed in the following decade. By 2010, 378 projects were implemented, 63 percent of which emerged from the original process.

Although deliberation is the main means of participation in more than half of all cases aimed at responsiveness, those innovations that rely on digital engagement are proliferating at a very fast pace. Between 2010 and 2015, 210 digital innovations were created to pursue responsiveness. While crowdsourced policymaking is increasingly used to enable citizens to play a more direct role in formulating policies, numerous policy platforms have been designed to close the gap between elected representatives and citizens. They enable citizens, for example, to track their representatives' everyday activities and legislative work, to send feedback, to suggest how they should vote on certain issues, besides allowing them to comment on existing bills of law and sending suggestions for new ones. Responsiveness-oriented digital platforms have been implemented both by governments and CSOs. On the government side, such platforms are usually developed and hosted by the legislatures themselves, as are, for example, Know your Deputy in Honduras, My Senate in Colombia, and E-Democracy in Brazil. On the civil society side, examples are Open Congress (Chile), SeamOs (Colombia), and Curul501 (Mexico). In Argentina, the platform Activate the Congress supported the green wave (*Marea Verde*) feminist movement in its pressure to approve the abortion law in 2020. The platform facilitates communication between citizens and policymakers by phone or via messages sent to their social media accounts. It has been accessed more than one million times, and nearly 200,000 messages have been sent to policymakers to pressure them to vote in favor of the abortion law.

5.2.3 Rule of Law

While democratic innovations aimed at strengthening the rule of law are comparatively very few, the range of problems they seek to address is quite broad. Four sets of problems, summarized in Table 3, can be identified based on the aims of such 374 innovations, namely, crime and lack of security; abuse of

Table 3 Innovations aimed at rule of law

Problems	Aims
Crime and lack of security	Curb crime and increase security Improve the state's security capacity Enforce the law
Abuse of state power and human rights violations	Monitor performance of police and security forces Control police brutality and corruption Protect human rights
Judicial ineffectiveness and unequal access to justice	Ensure transparent and accountable judicial institutions Ensure access to justice for low-income and less-educated people
Armed conflicts and peace	Resolve conflicts Develop peace strategies

state power and human rights violations; ineffective judiciary and unequal access to justice; and armed conflicts and peace. Despite so many problems, this is clearly the end which democratic innovations have been most ineffective in achieving, and few cases with positive outcomes have been observed.

Democratic innovations that deal with problems related to *crime and lack of security* seek to improve the state's security capacity by including citizens in all stages of the policy process, for example, identifying criminality problems present in their communities, providing community-managed security, and monitoring the implementation of security services and the performance of surveillance institutions. One rare successful example in this area was Honduras's Municipal Observatories for Coexistence and Citizen Security. These institutions, which combined citizen representation and deliberation, were implemented in 2014 in the thirty municipalities registering the highest levels of violence and criminality. They sought to generate evidence-based information in order to define actions focused on reducing violence and insecurity. The goal was to involve local citizens in the formulation, implementation, and evaluation of security policies tailored to their communities. Between 2015 and 2018, homicide levels decreased 34 percent in the municipalities where observatories were implemented, while homicide rates dropped only 13 percent in municipalities without observatories (UNDP Honduras, 2019).

Problems related to *abuse of state power and human rights violations* have been mostly addressed by democratic innovations promoted by CSOs, which increasingly relied on digital engagement. A variety of policy platforms have been designed to oversee police and security forces and intensify the implementation of existing laws and policies, particularly those intended to contain criminality and control abuses of state power. Often relying on geolocation, they address issues as diverse as gender violence, human rights violations, and drug-related violence.

Democratic innovations that are concerned with *judicial ineffectiveness and unequal access to justice* try to ensure more transparent and accountable judicial institutions. In Central America, some institutions of citizen oversight have combined citizen representation and deliberation to address issues such as judicial reform. One example is Guatemala's Observatory of the Criminal Justice System, a citizen oversight institution established in 2017 to scrutinize important judicial cases. The high hopes of making the judiciary more transparent by means of citizen participation quickly dissipated after the then incumbent president was himself investigated.

Finally, problems related to *armed conflicts and peace* are addressed by democratic innovations that engage in conflict resolution and develop peace strategies. In Colombia, numerous citizen oversight institutions and several deliberative innovations were active during the entire peace process. Both government and CSOs have experimented with innovative forms of conflict resolution, in addition to promoting deliberation of the terms of the peace agreement in "conversation tables" and "regional meetings for peace" across the country. No deliberation was enough, however, to bring the population to a consensus before the 2016 peace plebiscite.

5.2.4 Social Equality

Just like the deficits of representative democracy in Latin America cannot be dissociated from the (un)rule of law (O'Donnell, 2004), they are also strongly related to other structural problems such as inequality. Democratic innovations whose primary end is social equality aim to improve the living conditions, well-being, and capabilities of individuals, groups, and communities.

Democratic innovations seek to address three sets of problems related to inequality, summarized in Table 4. *Income inequality* was perhaps the first problem addressed by a democratic innovation and remains a central one. Since the widespread implementation of participatory budgeting in the 1990s, democratic innovations have been concerned with issues such as redistributive policies, the well-being of citizens, the improvement of their life conditions, economic and social rights, food and nutrition security, and poverty reduction. Democratic innovations also try to tackle problems related to *territorial inequality*, in particular those related to rural development, urban development

Table 4 Innovations aimed at social equality

Problems	Aims
Income inequality	Enhance the formulation and implementation of redistributive policies
	Ensure food and nutrition security
	Reduce poverty
Territorial inequality	Promote rural development, urban development (infrastructure), and
	sustainable development (environment)
Unequal access to social goods and services	Ensure and improve the provision of health, education, housing, water, and other social goods and services

(e.g., infrastructure), and sustainable development (e.g., environment). The *unequal access to social goods and services* is a constant problem addressed by democratic innovations. Many aim to improve the provision of health, education, housing, water, sanitation, and electricity, among others.

Democratic innovations that primarily seek to increase social equality very often combine political inclusion as their secondary end, which makes sense given that problems of inequality can hardly be dissociated from gender, racial, or ethnic discrimination. Such a combination of ends can be seen, for example, in innovations that seek to ensure the provision of health care to Indigenous peoples, boost the representation of black women, or promote the education of rural girls and adolescents. A well-known example is the local health councils in Brazil, which enable citizens in impoverished areas to gain access to the health system while improving the representation of historically excluded groups such as Afro-descendants (Coelho, 2007).

Democratic innovations aimed at enhancing social equality are mostly promoted by governments, take place at the local level, involve deliberation, and affect almost evenly all stages of the policy cycle except for evaluation.

Governments are the sole initiator of 44 percent of innovations related to social equality. When partnerships with CSOs, international organizations, or private stakeholders are taken into consideration, governments have been involved in 71 percent of equality-oriented innovations. While altogether 793 diverse innovations target social equality, several of them have been replicated hundreds or even thousands of times at the local level. This mostly applies to deliberative councils that allow citizens to deliberate on social policies, and management councils and participatory implementation processes that make sure those policies are executed as they should.

Due to the pioneering research on participatory budgeting, democratic innovations aimed at enhancing social equality have been investigated as case studies more often and therefore offer more evidence of impact. Extensive research has focused on participatory budgeting's ability to promote social justice by enabling greater participation of the poor (Abers, 1998) and the allocation of additional resources to areas with more poverty and less infrastructure (Wampler, 2007). Scholars argued that, among other things, it led to a more equitable redistribution of public goods, improved well-being, and increased participation among disadvantaged groups. In Brazil, in addition to including less-educated and lower-income citizens (Baiocchi, 2003), participatory budgeting has been associated with increased health-care spending and decreased infant mortality rates in the country's 253 largest cities (Touchton & Wampler, 2014). In its travels across Latin America, however, participatory budgeting lost its original social goals of redistribution and inclusion and became more of a tool for good governance (Ganuza & Baiocchi, 2012).

Yet the positive impact of democratic innovations on social equality extends beyond participatory budgeting. In Brazil, the combination of management councils, inclusive social programs, and state capacity has improved well-being by reducing infant and maternal mortality rates in addition to empowering women, encouraging school attendance, and increasing incomes (Wampler et al., 2019). In Guatemala, citizen assemblies brought Indigenous Mam people together with the government and CSOs to deliberate on issues related to water and sanitation services, ensuring their input in the formulation of three public policies for water and sanitation (UNDP, 2009). In Colombia, an experiment called Ideas for Change organized citizens from vulnerable communities into informal citizens' assemblies that sought to identify problems and seek innovative solutions together with local authorities and scientists, resulting in increased water access and improved water quality for 585 families in 11 communities, 40 percent of which were Indigenous and 60 percent of whom were peasants living in extreme poverty (Cinara, 2014). In Venezuela, despite the large setbacks seen later in this policy area, in the early 2000s health committees designed to include citizens in the planning, management, delivery, and monitoring of primary health-care services at the neighborhood level contributed to improving health access for 17 million people all over the country (Armada et al., 2009), in addition to engaging more than a million citizens in thousands of communal assemblies to deliberate on problems and priorities concerning their health (Muntaner et al., 2008).

However, those democratic innovations that achieve some improvements in social equality are not free of shortcomings. Poverty itself is a known constraint on participation. In Uruguay, while a relatively successful participatory decentralization process put forward by the leftist Broad Front in Montevideo managed to redistribute resources to the poor in some neighborhoods (Goldfrank, 2011), poverty limited citizen participation, divided residents, and undermined community cooperation and solidarity (Canel, 2010: 4). Moreover, the very success of a democratic innovation may hinder its sustainability. In Mexico, the initial triumph of participatory water management in two cities turned citizens' assemblies into venues of dissent, transformed participants into local power brokers, threatened the power of local elected officials, and became a political liability (Herrera, 2017).

5.2.5 Political Inclusion

Closely connected to the problems associated with inequality are those related to so-called low-intensity citizenship (O'Donnell, 1993). Democratic innovations that seek to increase political inclusion address the large presence of historically marginalized groups in Latin America, their need for recognition and empowerment, and the structural discrimination they suffer.

The political inclusion of women, LGBT people, Afro descendants, Indigenous peoples, people with disabilities, elderly people, and young people is sought by democratic innovations that aim at enforcing the political rights and protecting the cultural rights of those groups, ensuring they receive fair treatment, enhancing their capabilities, improving their access to public services, and protecting them from police violence and all sorts of discrimination (see Table 5). Democratic innovations whose primary end is political inclusion are mostly implemented by

Table 5 Innovations aimed at political inclusion

Problems	Aims
Gender discrimination	Enhance recognition of, provide representation for, and fight discrimination against women and LGBT people Expand gender rights
Racial discrimination	Enhance recognition and cultural rights of, provide representation for, and fight discrimination against Afro-descendants
Ethnic discrimination	Enhance recognition and cultural rights of and provide representation for Indigenous peoples Protect Indigenous lands and natural resources
Age or disability discrimination	Expand policies for young people or the elderly Further inclusion of people with disabilities

governments; are well distributed at the local, regional, and national levels; have mostly citizen representation as a primary means of participation; and are particularly present at the agenda-setting stage of the policy cycle.

Governments at all levels have been involved in as much as 78 percent of democratic innovations aimed at enhancing political inclusion, very frequently through the creation of representative councils, where members of historically marginalized groups have a seat and are thus able to speak on behalf of and stand for the interests and values of the groups they claim to represent. In such participatory institutions, those groups set the agenda for policies that enhance their recognition, fight discrimination against them, and expand their political and cultural rights. By means of nonelectoral citizen representation, representative councils can potentially reduce deficits of representation resulting from elections by ensuring the presence in the policy process of groups that are rarely, if ever, able to elect officials who will advocate for their specific interests.

Although democratic innovations seek to cover a vast array of problems related to political exclusion, they are far from numerous or effective enough to deal with the difficulties faced by those groups that comprise millions of people who are highly discriminated against and vastly underrepresented. Those innovations try to ensure the presence of those groups in existing political institutions or create new institutions and processes where they are entitled to set the agenda and formulate policies attentive to their specific identities and interests as groups. Yet the impact of these innovations remains limited.

Democratic innovations addressing the youth, women, and LGBT people have grown rapidly in number in recent years and cut across all four means of participation. As many as 202 designs focus on the inclusion of young people, 60 percent of which have been implemented since 2010. Except for twenty cases that rely primarily on digital engagement (a rather low proportion given the target group), all others rely equally on deliberation and citizen representation. A total of 27 percent of these innovations have resulted in policies or laws devoted to the youth.

As for women, 166 democratic innovations have been created since 1990, 68 percent of which after 2010. Only between 2014 and 2020 as many as eighty-six new designs were implemented across the eighteen countries, most of which involving the civil society. Some participatory institutions created by governments have been, however, central in pushing further innovation. In Uruguay, for example, since the National Institute for Women (Inmujeres, a representative council) was founded in 2005, several laws and policies targeting women's needs and interests have been drafted through participatory processes. Democratic innovations have also walked hand-in-hand with the mobilization and digital activism of women. Since 2016, when the recent feminist wave began with #NiUnaMenos, thirty-four democratic innovations based on digital engagement have been created addressing issues such as gender-based harassment, violence, and discrimination. Gender inclusion has been also increasingly pursued by democratic innovations targeting LGBT people. Out of a total of nineteen designs, twelve have been created since 2010.

By contrast, democratic innovations concerned with black people and Indigenous peoples grow at a slower pace. In a region where one in four citizens identify as Afro-descendant, only twenty-four participatory innovations dealing with this group were implemented over thirty years, mostly in Brazil and Colombia, the countries with the largest such populations. Out of these twenty-four designs, only three have positively impacted on political inclusion. While as many as 129 democratic innovations targeting Indigenous peoples were created (some of them replicated numerous times, like prior consultations), about half of them (67) have achieved some degree of political inclusion. However, existing case studies point out serious problems in their implementation. In prior consultations, for example, power and information asymmetries put strong constraints on deliberation. In Peru, Indigenous peoples' difficulties to articulate their visions and demands limited the effectiveness of this participatory institution (Flemmer & Schilling-Vacaflor, 2016). Moreover, the lack of incorporation of those groups in the regulation and implementation of prior consultations limits their institutional strength. In Ecuador, weak ties between Indigenous movements and the government turned prior consultations into weak institutions (Falleti & Riofrancos, 2018).

5.3 The Impact of Democratic Innovations

While there has been extensive research on democratic innovations, fewer efforts have been directed toward investigating their impact. Most investigations on impact comprise case studies, and not much comparative research has been undertaken across designs and countries (Ryan, 2021). Pursuing large-N research on democratic innovations is indeed very challenging. While there is limited reliable evidence of impact, existing research tends to emphasize successful cases (Spada and Ryan, 2017). Consequently, the variables of the LATINNO dataset that measure impact contain several missing values and a possible bias toward positive results.

Out of 3,181 cases with available reliable evidence, as much as 77 percent of democratic innovations across the eighteen countries have fully achieved the *aims* they were purportedly designed for (for example, drafting a policy, enacting a law, preparing a budget, providing recommendations). While this does not imply that such aims have been successfully attained according to normative democratic standards (e.g., legitimacy, justice, inclusiveness), this indicates that most democratic innovations are highly effectively carried out. Indeed, according to the existing evidence (N = 2,274), only 6 percent of democratic innovations in Latin America did not engender some sort of *output* (e.g., policy draft, law draft, recommendations, guidelines, reports, plans). Out of 1,189 democratic innovations that had as outputs drafts of policies or laws and for which there is reliable evidence available, 91 percent have in fact enacted or implemented them (i.e., resulted in an *outcome*). Hence, considering the entire dataset (N = 3,713), less than one-third (29 percent) of all democratic innovations implemented in Latin America between 1990 and 2020 resulted in an enacted law or implemented policy. Most of these are concentrated in Brazil, Argentina, and Colombia, which are also the countries with the highest number of democratic innovations.

But to what extent have democratic innovations in Latin America achieved their *ends*, that is, improved accountability or responsiveness, strengthened the rule or law, or increased social equality or political inclusion? Among cases with reliable evidence (N = 1,597), exactly 50 percent have fully accomplished their ends, 47 percent have had their ends partially fulfilled, and only 3 percent have had no impact at all (see Figure 14). While the absence of reliable evidence to assess whether one or more of the ends pursued by democratic innovations has been achieved does not indicate absence of impact, it is fair to say that 42 percent of all democratic innovations in Latin America have achieved their ends to some extent (22 percent fully and 20 percent partially).

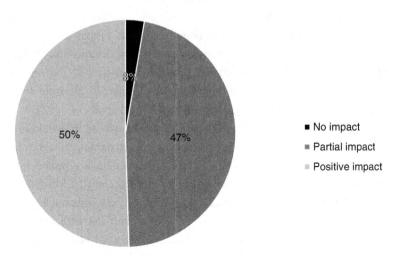

Figure 14 Impact on ends of democratic innovations

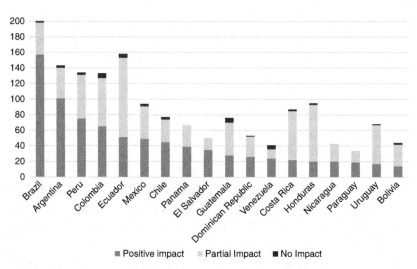

Figure 15 Impact on ends across countries

The 807 democratic innovations that fully achieved their ends are concentrated in Brazil, Argentina, and Peru, as shown in Figure 15. Their success is explained by a combination of contextual factors, institutional aspects, and design features (Pogrebinschi & Acosta, 2023). Mostly located in Ecuador, Honduras, and Costa Rica, the 746 democratic innovations which had a partial impact comprise cases that have not completely achieved ends as intended by designers, or cases designed to pursue more than one end and which haven't attained them all. For example, Colombia's Guarantees National Table sought to strengthen the rule of law by protecting human rights, and while it was successful in achieving significant agreements and actions, it failed to reduce the number of attacks against human rights activists (Tapia & Hernández, 2016). The forty-four democratic innovations that have demonstrably failed to fulfill their ends are predominantly in Colombia, Guatemala, Ecuador, and Venezuela. Those innovations that produced no impact at all were for the most part implemented by governments at the national level.

Governments were involved in 81 percent of democratic innovations that fully achieved their ends, indicating that state-led citizen participation may have a higher chance of impact. Nonetheless, among democratic innovations implemented by civil society with no government involvement and for which there is evidence of impact available, 53 percent fully achieved their ends and 45 percent were partially successful in this regard. More than half (54 percent) of fully impactful democratic innovations have been implemented at the local level, while about one-third (32 percent) of them took place at the national level.

Interestingly, only 29 percent of fully impactful democratic innovations were embedded in laws or constitutions; most of them (52 percent) were created by governmental actions or programs, which can be easily revoked. This is consistent with the fact that 46 percent of fully impactful innovations were processes, while only 31 percent were institutions.

The democratic innovations that achieved a higher degree of impact sought to increase responsiveness or social equality (see Figure 16). Democratic innovations that only partially fulfilled their ends were also mainly aimed at enhancing social equality or responsiveness. As for democratic innovations that failed to have an impact on their ends, they focused primarily on enhancing political inclusion or responsiveness. Deliberation was the primary means of participation in more than half (53 percent) of innovations that fully fulfilled their ends.

The data certainly do not imply that democratic innovations successfully solved broad public problems and therewith increased the quality of democracy in given countries. Yet, it indicates that democratic innovations may have an impact on democratic qualities when they fully achieve their ends. Guatemala's National Dialogue on HIV and Human Rights in 2013 might not have eliminated gender discrimination, but it was considered crucial for the introduction of several legislative bills and the creation of the Office on Sexual and Gender Diversity in 2014 (UNDP, 2014), and hence it has accomplished some political inclusion. Also in Guatemala, Community-led Total Sanitation (SANTOLIC) may not have solved the country's unequal access to social goods and services, but the 243 communities that actively engaged in implementing and monitoring

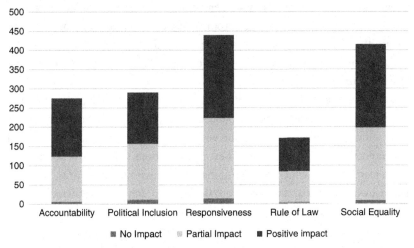

Figure 16 Ends of democratic innovations with impact

sanitation actions improved the sanitation of 4,751 families (Helvetas & UNICEF, 2018), and to an extent achieved social equality.

6 Is There Still Room for Innovation in Latin America?

When the third wave of democracy hit Latin America in the late 1970s, scholars expected representative institutions to solve the political and social problems engrained after so many years of authoritarian rule. However, where representative institutions were expected to consolidate, participatory innovations started to proliferate after the 1990s. As the region struggled with low levels of accountability and responsiveness, a flawed rule of law, and very high levels of social inequality and political exclusion, governments and CSOs increasingly experimented with new ways of combining representation with participation.

Failing to follow the liberal script, democracy in Latin America wrote a narrative of its own. This narrative can be read in different ways, but none should ignore the role played by the institutions, processes, and mechanisms of citizen participation. These democratic innovations may not have always been novel or truly democratic. Not all of them worked well or had any meaningful impact. Some of them have remained simple pieces of paper, never becoming anything more than unfulfilled promises in laws and constitutions. Others may have become quite solid institutions, engaged thousands of citizens over several years, and generated dozens of responsive policies, only to be dismantled with a single decree from a newly elected president. Yet democratic innovations are part and parcel of Latin America's democracy, and they are too numerous to be ignored, regardless of how many have failed or not lived up to their promise.

This Element has presented a comprehensive and comparative picture that reveals the breadth and variety of democratic innovations in Latin America based on original data collected from 3,744 cases across 18 countries for a period of 30 years. These data have allowed me to paint the empirical landscape of three decades of democratic innovation in the region, indicating how the latter has been facilitated by at least five – often intertwined – aspects, namely democratization, constitutionalization, decentralization, the left turn, and digitalization. I have also introduced an empirically grounded concept of democratic innovations, taking issue with prevailing understandings. I argued that democratic innovations extend beyond institutions to include processes and mechanisms, all of which may be initiated by governments, CSOs, or international organizations, and which are designed to enhance democracy, rather than simply increase citizen participation.

At the core of the analysis offered by this Element lies the empirical observation that democratic innovations in Latin America rely on multiple combinations of means of participation and ends of innovations. Based on this insight, I have developed a typology of democratic innovations structured around the four means of citizen participation that have evolved in eighteen Latin American countries since 1990, namely, deliberation, citizen representation, digital engagement, and direct voting. The typology comprises altogether twenty subtypes of democratic innovations, which encompass the rich variety of institutions, processes, and mechanisms of citizen participation.

One of the main claims of this Element is that democratic innovations do not simply aim to increase citizen participation; they seek rather to enhance democracy. The inclusion of citizens in policy processes is a necessary condition, but not a sufficient one to ensure that innovations are properly participatory or that they yield democratic results – meaning results that improve the quality of democracy. I argue that democratic innovations may improve democracy when they are designed such that they – by means of citizen participation – advance at least one of five ends that reflect different dimensions or qualities of democracy, namely, accountability, responsiveness, rule of law, social equality, and political inclusion. Each of these five ends relates to diverse sets of problems that democratic innovations seek to address.

I hence defend a problem-driven approach to democratic innovations, in which means of participation and ends of innovation combine to address public problems. These problems can in a broader perspective be related to challenges faced by democracy in Latin America, such as deficits of representation, the (un)rule of law, and inequality. This is the backdrop of what I elsewhere called pragmatic democracy, and in this Element refer to as Latin America's democratic experimentalism.

An important step toward properly understanding and assessing democratic innovations is to move beyond the idea that they are meant to impact decision-making or must do so in order to be effective. One of the contributions of this Element is to call attention to four moments at which democracy can be improved by means of citizen participation, relating them to each stage of the policy cycle. Democratic innovations matter for democracy and may impact policies regardless of whether citizens are entitled to take political decisions. There is plenty of evidence of how citizen participation is an asset to all four stages of the policy cycle, each stage critical to ensuring that policies can effectively address the intended problems. For instance, a political decision matters only if it is implemented and enforced, and citizen participation has proved crucial for the execution and monitoring of policies, especially in contexts of low state capacity, as in Latin America. Therefore, neither should the effectiveness of democratic innovations and their impact on democracy be measured simply by their ability to produce decisions, nor should their success be gauged by the number of policies produced via citizen participation.

Yet if democratic innovations had been entirely effective and had all worked as expected, could recent democratic backslides in Latin America have been prevented? Was the belief in participatory policymaking abandoned with the electoral rejection of leftist governments in several countries? Were the massive protests in the recent past in numerous countries an indication of the inability of democratic innovations to function as channels of communication between governments and citizens, having failed to enable citizens to voice their needs and demands?

These questions point to a new research agenda and cannot be answered in this conclusion. Nevertheless, a brief look at Brazil may offer some clues and provide food for thought to reflect on other countries. Why did the country, once the "laboratory of democratic innovations" toward which, as recently as 2011, "many of us may soon turn our eyes . . . to understand their accomplishments in democratic governance" (Fung, 2011: 857), so quickly kneel down to an authoritarian-populist government that loathes citizen participation? How could Brazil's vast architecture of participatory institutions be so easily demolished by a single presidential decree?

The data offer four reasons why even apparently stable participatory institutions such as national councils in Brazil collapsed after right-wing president Bolsonaro declared their extinction in April 2019. First, *democratic innovation was mostly state-driven.* Since 1990, democratic innovations in Brazil have emerged almost exclusively upon the government's initiative, not always involving civil society in their implementation. Until the end of 2015, when the impeachment process of former president Rousseff began, 67 percent of all democratic innovations in the country were convened alone by governments at the local, regional, or national levels. Soon after the impeachment, internal rules of participatory institutions were changed, civil society representatives were displaced, and resources were cut by the new government while civil society could do nothing to avoid this (Pogrebinschi & Tanscheit, 2017a). Second, *democratic innovations were seldom formalized.* Within the same period, 65 percent of democratic innovations with government involvement were created or adopted through executive administrative acts or governmental programs, which can be easily revoked as governments change. No more than 27 percent had been incorporated in legislation or in the constitution. A remaining 8 percent had no formalization at all. Third, *the outputs of democratic innovations were almost never binding.* Until 2015, 73 percent of democratic innovations in Brazil had some sort of output, for example, the drafting of policies or recommendations for policy formulation. However, only

14 percent of outputs were binding, meaning that authorities were hardly ever compelled to implement or incorporate the outputs of citizen participation. Fourth, *the impact of democratic innovations on the enactment of policies was relatively low.* Although some important laws resulted from citizen participation at the national level, less than half of Brazil's democratic innovations have actually affected the adoption of new policies.

This cautionary tale speaks to what makes democratic innovations weak and what could make them stronger. The limited involvement of civil society in implementation, low levels of formalization, lack of bindingness, and low impact all seem to weaken democratic innovations. Their relative ineffectiveness has possibly contributed to institutional weakness, as political and social actors have probably lacked interest in enforcing innovations when challenged. At the end of 2015, Brazil had more than 200 active democratic innovations, of which 121 were institutions. Four years later, 147 of these innovations were still active, 100 of which were institutions. Brazil's Supreme Court ruling on Bolsonaro's decree implied that democratic innovations grounded in law or in the constitution could not be extinguished. Yet Bolsonaro still managed to cut resources, manipulate internal rules, and control CSO access to those institutions that survived, leaving them emptied and soulless. Not even the constitution protects institutions from presidents in Latin America.

Likewise, in Ecuador, once the epitome of democratic innovation under the left turn, the constitutional status of participatory institutions has proven worthless in protecting them against the region's hyper-presidentialism. The Council for Citizen Participation and Social Control was established, according to the then new 2008 Constitution, to "promote public participation and encourage public deliberation." It soon became clear that deliberation was not going to function as defined in the 2010 Citizen Participation Law: "the dialogical processing of the relations and conflicts between state and society." Successive conflicts and lack of dialogue rendered understanding between government and civil society impossible, and the Council became an instrument to expand the power of the executive branch (Balderacchi, 2015).

The deliberative wave that hit Latin America in the early 1990s and evolved until it reached a peak as several countries in the region surfed the pink tide has clearly receded since 2015. First, deliberative innovations became increasingly less deliberative and unable to fulfill their democratic promise. On top of that, elected governments that followed those of the left turn drastically slowed down the implementation of democratic innovations, especially those based on deliberation.

By 2019, not only did the left appear to have declined, but a turn to the right was a concrete fear throughout the region. The "*annus horribilis*" for democracy in Latin America was likewise horrible for democratic innovation. Virtually all types of democratic innovations experienced a hasty decline. The total number of democratic innovations created in 2019 across the eighteen countries was much lower than in previous years, and several countries, besides Brazil, saw participatory institutions shut down and participatory processes interrupted. At least 800 democratic innovations were discontinued in Latin America between 2015 and 2019.[9] One could almost wonder whether democratic innovation had come to an end alongside the left turn or whether they were dying out together with democracy.

The year 2020 started with a deadly pandemic that soon had Latin America as its epicenter. Nonetheless, in this region of so many contradictions, despite so many restrictions imposed by the health emergency for two long years, citizens took the streets to protest, faced long lines at polling stations to elect the left again, and, especially, relied on digital technology to bring democratic innovation back to life.

The COVID-19 pandemic had an enormous impact on democratic innovation in Latin America. In 2020, 125 democratic innovations specifically designed to address problems resulting from the pandemic were created across the 18 countries. This number is almost as high as the average number of democratic innovations created in the region in each of the previous three years. Moreover, 54 percent of those democratic innovations were introduced by civil society organizations, 84 percent of which had no government involvement at all. It likely comes as no surprise that 75 percent of democratic innovations addressing the COVID-19 pandemic rely on digital engagement as their primary means of participation.

Instead of being an outlier, 2020 has deepened and confirmed two trends already evident within the data in the previous decade.

First, *civil society is taking the lead in democratic innovation, and citizen participation in Latin America is becoming less state-driven*. Between 2011 and 2016, the number of innovations promoted by CSOs grew 31 percent per year, while government-led innovations grew at a slower pace of 10 percent per year. In 2020, the number of democratic innovations created by civil society was 62 percent higher than the number civil society created in 2010. The expansion of civil society leadership follows the slow retreat of the state. Between 2018 and 2020, governments were responsible for creating alone an average of seventy democratic innovations per year throughout the region, while civil society organizations were involved in the creation of sixty-seven. Just ten

---

[9] One should keep in mind that this number includes participatory mechanisms that are meant to be short-lived.

years earlier, between 2008 and 2010, governments created an average of eighty-one democratic innovations per year, and civil society only thirty-six.

Second, *digital engagement is expanding rapidly, while other means of citizen participation are hardly expanding at all.* Between 2008 and 2016, the number of digital-based democratic innovations grew at an average rate of 48 percent per year. Conversely, in the same period, the number of democratic innovations relying on citizen representation and deliberation each increased by only 9 percent per year. As much as 67 percent of all innovations created in 2020 in Latin America relied on digital engagement as a primary or secondary means of citizen participation.

These trends were already underway before the COVID-19 pandemic and are not merely a result of the state's retreat and deliberation's decline after the end of the left turn in 2015. Considering all digital democratic innovations implemented in Latin America over the thirty years analyzed in this Element, more than half (54 percent) had no involvement at all from governments; by contrast, less than a quarter of democratic innovations that relied on the other three means of participation emerged and functioned without government involvement. Considering that digitalization started to intensify only after 2010, it becomes even more clear how it is the main driver behind civil society's increasing role in the promotion of democratic innovations.

Because digital innovations require relatively fewer resources and less infrastructure to set up, CSOs depend to a lesser extent on governments to promote citizen participation. Moreover, the data also show that CSOs seeking to implement digital democratic innovations tend to partner with international organizations more often than with governments. Nonetheless, just like other democratic innovations, those that rely on digital engagement are designed to impact public policies, and thus it is crucial that governments pick up on their outputs.

Yet, while digitalization expands and multiplies the opportunities for citizen participation, it also faces serious challenges, some of which are critical in Latin America, as several researchers have warned. First, digital engagement may have exclusionary effects. New technologies may amplify existing participatory biases by favoring the participation of male, higher income, or more highly educated citizens (Peixoto & Sifry, 2017). Second, their success may be hindered by the cultural and social contexts of some countries, in addition to technical deficiencies in design and implementation (Breuer & Welp, 2014). Finally, digital tools may not be able to deliver proper democratic results. Regardless of good design and active participation, digital-based participatory processes can still result in policies strongly influenced by lobbyists and privileged interests (Alsina & Martí, 2018).

Nonetheless, the two trends identified in this conclusion tend to reinforce each other: digitalization enables CSO-initiated innovations, and CSOs push digital innovations. With digital innovations being more restricted to participatory mechanisms and processes, the number of participatory institutions is likely to further decrease, regardless of whether governments are for or against citizen participation.

If these trends are confirmed, a change seems to be underway in Latin America. While democratic innovation in the region since 1990 has been mostly the work of state-driven, participatory institutions that relied on deliberation, the future of citizen participation seems to belong to digital mechanisms and processes initiated by civil society. One can only hope that this new wave of democratic experimentalism pushes for more accountable and responsive political institutions, and more equal and inclusive democracy.

List of Democratic Innovations Cited

Activate the Congress, Argentina, 2018. In: https://latinno.net/en/case/1151/

An Eye on the Vote, Argentina, 2015. In: https://latinno.net/en/case/1058/

Bacheando, Paraguay, 2015. In: https://latinno.net/en/case/16024/

Bogotá Citizen Assembly, Colombia, 2020. In: https://latinno.net/en/case/5273/

Citizen Initiative "Law 3 of 3", Mexico, 2016. In: https://latinno.net/en/case/13131/

Citizens' Assembly Against Corruption, Chihuahua, Mexico, 2020. In: https://secretaria.anticorrupcion.org/wp-content/uploads/2021/02/Ficha_Metodolog%C3%ADa_del_Jurado_Ciudadano_y_ajustes_metodológicos.pdf

Clean Record, Brazil, 1997. In: https://latinno.net/en/case/3192/

Community-led Total Sanitation (SANTOLIC),Guatemala, 2016. In: https://latinno.net/en/case/10169/

Council to Home, Colombia, 2020. In: https://latinno.net/en/case/5346/

Curul 501, Mexico, 2011. In: https://latinno.net/en/case/13211/

Democracy OS, Argentina, 2014. In: https://latinno.net/en/case/1173/

E-Democracy, Brazil, 2009. In: https://latinno.net/en/case/3157/

Elderly Citizens' Council, Chile, 2018. In: https://latinno.net/en/case/4164/

Environmental Agenda for Water, Costa Rica, 2004. In: https://latinno.net/en/case/6116/

Eye Guate, Guatemala, 2014. In: https://latinno.net/en/case/10068/

First National Dialogue, Bolivia, 1997. In: https://latinno.net/en/case/2001/

Gender Violence Map, Brazil, 2019. In: https://latinno.net/en/case/3298/

Grand National Dialogue, Honduras, 2015. In: https://latinno.net/en/case/12013/

Health Committees, Venezuela, 2003. In: https://latinno.net/en/case/19006/

How Are We Doing? Cities Network, Colombia, 1998. In: https://latinno.net/en/case/5015/

Ideas for Change, Colombia, 2012. In: https://latinno.net/en/case/5163/

Indigenous Peoples' Advisory and Participatory Council, Argentina, 2016. In: https://latinno.net/en/case/1252/

InfoAmazonia, Brazil, 2014. In: https://latinno.net/en/case/3002/

InfoAmazonia, Colombia, 2012. In: https://latinno.net/en/case/5248/

Internet Civic Framework, Brazil, 2009. In: https://latinno.nct/en/case/3009/

Know your Deputy, Honduras, 2014. In: https://latinno.net/en/case/12057/

Local Observatories Bogotá, Colombia, 2011. In: https://latinno.net/en/case/5179/

Mapathon for Guapi, Colombia, 2016. In: https://latinno.net/en/case/5145/

Mapee, Colombia, 2018. In: https://latinno.net/en/case/5250/

Municipal Health Councils, Brazil, 1990. In: https://latinno.net/en/case/3142/

Municipal Observatories for Coexistence and Citizen Security, Honduras, 2014. In: https://latinno.net/en/case/12115/

My Senate, Colombia, 2017. In: https://latinno.net/en/case/5208/

National Committee Against Racism and All Forms of Discrimination, Bolivia, 2010. In: https://latinno.net/en/case/2087/

National Council for Children and Adolescents, Costa Rica, 1998. In: https://latinno.net/en/case/6032/

National Council for the Integration of Persons with Disabilities, Peru, 1999. In: https://latinno.net/en/case/17093/

National Council of Anti-discrimination and Pro-Human Rights of Lesbians, Gays, Bisexuals, Transvestites and Transsexuals, Brazil, 2001. In: https://latinno.net/en/case/3080/

National Council of Education, El Salvador, 2015. In: https://latinno.net/en/case/9020/

National Dialogue for Employment, Uruguay, 2011. In: https://latinno.net/en/case/18048/

National Dialogue for Justice Reform, Guatemala, 2016. In: https://latinno.net/en/case/10061/

National Dialogue on Climate Change, Ecuador, 2013. In: https://latinno.net/en/case/8086/

National Dialogue on HIV and Human Rights, Dominican Republic, 2013. In: https://latinno.net/en/case/7053/

National Dialogue on HIV and Human Rights, Guatemala, 2013. In: https://latinno.net/en/case/10118/

National Gender Council (INMUJERES), Uruguay, 2007. In: https://latinno.net/en/case/18018/

National Guarantees Table, Colombia, 2009. In: https://latinno.net/en/case/5199/

National Socio-Environmental Monitoring Committees, Bolivia, 2007. In: https://latinno.net/en/case/2010/

National Youth Council, Panama, 1998. In: https://latinno.net/en/case/15152/

Neighborhood Assemblies, Argentina, 2001. In: https://latinno.net/en/case/1003/

Neighborhoods in Action, Chile, 2015. In: https://latinno.net/en/case/4107/

Observatory of the Criminal Justice System, Guatemala, 2017. In: https://latinno.net/en/case/10014/

Open Congress, Chile, 2015. In: https://latinno.net/en/case/4110/

Participatory Strategic Plan of Santa Tecla, El Salvador, 2002. In: https://latinno.net/en/case/9015/

Plebiscite for Peace, Colombia, 2016. In: https://latinno.net/en/case/5151/

Plebiscite on Constitutional Reform, Chile, 2020. In: https://latinno.net/en/case/4142/

Popular Public Consultation on Water in Cochabamba, Bolivia, 1999. In: https://latinno.net/en/case/2008/

Qali Warma, Peru, 2012. In: https://latinno.net/en/case/17021/

Recall Referendum by Popular Mandate, Bolivia, 2009. In: https://latinno.net/en/case/2072/

SeamOs, Colombia, 2016. In: https://latinno.net/en/case/5138/

The Chile That We Want: Citizen Consultation, Chile, 2019. In: https://latinno.net/en/case/4152/

The Chile That We Want: Citizen Dialogues, Chile, 2019. In: https://latinno.net/en/case/4151/

Water Systems Administrative Boards, Honduras, 2006. In: https://latinno.net/en/case/12037/

We Have to Talk About Chile: Citizen Consultations, Chile, 2020. In: https://latinno.net/en/case/4189/

We Have to Talk About Chile: Digital Talks, Chile, 2020. In: https://latinno.net/en/case/4188/

Youth Action Plans, Uruguay, 2008. In: https://latinno.net/en/case/18021/

Youth Concertation Table, Nicaragua, 2014. In: https://latinno.net/en/case/14063/

References

Abers, R. (1998). From clientelism to cooperation: Local government, participatory policy, and civic organizing in Porto Alegre, Brazil. *Politics & Society*, **26**(4), 511–537.

Abers, R., & Keck, M. E. (2013). *Practical Authority: Agency and Institutional Change in Brazilian Water Politics*. Oxford: Oxford University Press.

Abramovay, P. (2017). *Sistemas deliberativos e processo decisório congressual: Um estudo sobre a aprovação do Marco Civil da Internet*. Doctoral Dissertation. Rio de Janeiro: Instituto de Estudos Sociais e Políticos of the State University of Rio de Janeiro.

Aitamurto, T., & Landemore, H. E. (2015). Five design principles for crowdsourced policymaking. *Journal of Social Media for Organizations*, **2**(1),1–19.

Alsina, V., & Martí, J. L. (2018). The birth of the CrowdLaw movement: Tech-based citizen participation, legitimacy and the quality of lawmaking. *Analyse & Kritik*, 40(2), 337–358.

Altman, D. (2011). *Direct Democracy Worldwide*. Cambridge: Cambridge University Press.

Altschuler, D., & Corrales, J. (2013). *The Promise of Participation: Experiments in Participatory Governance in Honduras and Guatemala*. London: Palgrave Macmillan.

Ansell, C. (2011). *Pragmatist Democracy*. New York, NY: Oxford University Press.

Arendt, H. (1970). *On Violence*. Boston: Houghton Mifflin Harcourt.

Armada, F., Muntaner, C., Chung, H., Williams-Brennan, L., & Benach, J. (2009). Barrio Adentro and the reduction of health inequalities in Venezuela. *International Journal of Health Services*, **39**(1), 161–187.

Avritzer, L. (2002). *Democracy and the Public Space in Latin America*. Princeton: Princeton University Press.

Avritzer, L. (2009). *Participatory Institutions in Democratic Brazil*. Baltimore: John Hopkins University Press.

Avritzer, L. (2017). *The Two Sides of Institutional Innovation: Promises and Limits of Democratic Participation in Latin America*. Cheltenham: Edward Elgar.

Baiocchi, G. (2003). *Radicals in Power: The Workers' Party and Experiments in Urban Democracy in Brazil*. London: Zed Books.

Baiocchi, G., & Ganuza, E. (2017). *Popular Democracy. The Paradox of Participation*. Stanford: Stanford University Press.

Balderacchi, C. (2015). Participatory mechanisms in Bolivia, Ecuador and Venezuela: Deepening or undermining democracy? *Government and Opposition*, **52**(1), 131–161.

Bohman, J. (1998). Survey article: The coming of age of deliberative democracy. *The Journal of Political Philosophy*, 6(4), 400–425.

Breuer, A. (2007). Institutions of direct democracy and accountability in Latin America's presidential democracies. *Democratization*, **14**(4), 554–579.

Breuer, A., & Welp, Y. (2014). Digital trends in Latin American politics (1990–2012). In A. Breuer and Y. Welp, eds., *Digital Technologies for Democratic Governance in Latin America: Opportunities and Risks*. London: Routledge, pp. 1–16.

Cameron, M. A., Hershberg, E., & Sharpe, K. (2012). *New Institutions for Participatory Democracy in Latin America*. New York: Palgrave Macmillan.

Canel, E. (2010). *Barrio Democracy in Latin America: Participatory Decentralization and Community Activism in Montevideo*. University Park: Penn State University Press.

Cinara. (2014). *Levantamiento de línea base, sistematización y evaluación de los proyectos seleccionados de Ideas para el Cambio 2012*. Cali: Universidad del Valle.

Coelho, V. S. P. (2007). Brazilian health councils: Including the excluded? In A. Cornwall & V. S. P. Coelho eds., *Spaces for Change?* London: Zed Books, 33–54.

Collado, A. (2018). Las políticas públicas de participación ciudadana en Chile. *Revista Estudios de Políticas Públicas*, **4**(1), 79–98.

Collier, D., & Levitsky, S. (2009). Conceptual hierarchies in comparative research: The case of democracy. In D. Collier and J. Gerring, eds., *Concepts and Method in Social Science: The Tradition of Giovanni Sartori*. London: Routledge, 269–288.

Collier, D., LaPorte, J., & Seawright, J. (2008). Putting typologies to work: Concept formation, measurement, and analytic rigor. *Political Research Quarterly*, **65**(1), 217–232.

Cornwall, A., & Coelho, V. S. (2007). *Spaces for Change? The Politics of Citizen Participation in New Democratic Arenas*, Vol. 4. London: Zed Books.

Dagnino, E. (2010). Civil society in Latin America: Participatory citizens or service providers? In H. Moksnes and M. Melin, eds., *Power to the People? (Con-)tested Civil Society in Search of Democracy*. Uppsala: Uppsala University, 23–39.

Dagnino, E., Olvera, A., & Panfichi, A. (2008). Democratic innovation in Latin America: A first look at the democratic participatory project. In D. Evelina,

O. Alberto, and P. Aldo, eds., *Democratic Innovation in the South*. Buenos Aires: Consejo Latinoamericano de Ciencias Sociales, 27–46.

Dewey, J. (1939). *The Public and its Problems*. Chicago: University of Chicago Press.

Donaghy, M. M. (2013). *Civil Society and Participatory Governance: Municipal Councils and Social Housing Programs in Brazil*. London: Routledge.

Dryzek, J. S. (2007). Theory, evidence, and the tasks of deliberation. In S. Rosenberg, ed., *Deliberation, Participation and Democracy*. London: Palgrave Macmillan, 237–250.

Durán-Martínez, A. (2012). Presidents, parties, and referenda in Latin America. *Comparative Political Studies*, **45**(9), 1159–1187.

Elstub, S., & Escobar, O. (2019). Defining and typologising democratic innovations. In S. Elstub and O. Escobar, eds., *Handbook of Democratic Innovation and Governance*. Cheltenham: Edward Elgar, 11–31.

Falleti, T. G., & Cunial, S. L. (2018). *Participation in Social Policy: Public Health in Comparative Perspective*. Cambridge: Cambridge University Press.

Falleti, T. G., & Riofrancos, T. (2018). Endogenous participation: Strengthening prior consultation in extractive economies. *World Politics*, **70**(1), 86–121.

FAO [Food and Agriculture Organization], IFAD [International Fund for Agricultural Development] & WFP [World Food Programme]. (2013). The State of Food Insecurity in the World: The Multiple Dimensions of Food Security. Rome: FAO.

Fiorini, E. (2015). *COPISA in Ecuador: Participation that Wasn't*. Master's Thesis. Tucson: Graduate College of Latin American Studies, University of Arizona.

Flemmer, R., & Schilling-Vacaflor, A. (2016). Unfulfilled promises of the consultation approach: The limits to effective indigenous participation in Bolivia's and Peru's extractive industries. *Third World Quarterly*, **37**(1), 172–88.

Frega, R. (2019). *Pragmatism and the Wide View of Democracy*. Cham: Palgrave Macmillan.

Fung, A. (2003). Recipes for public spheres: Eight institutional design choices and their consequences. *Journal of Political Philosophy*, **1**(3), 338–67.

Fung, A. (2006). Varieties of participation in complex governance. *Public Administration Review*, **66**(1), 66–75.

Fung, A. (2011). Reinventing democracy in Latin America. *Perspective on Politics*, **9**(4), 857–71.

Fung, A. (2012). Continuous institutional innovation and the pragmatic conception of democracy. *Polity*, **44**(4), 609–624.

Fung, A. (2015). Putting the public back into governance: The challenges of citizen participation and its future. *Public Administration Review*, **75**(4), 513–22.

Fung, A., & Wright, R. O. (2003). *Deepening Democracy: Institutional Innovations in Empowered Participatory Governance*. London: Verso.

Ganuza, E., & Baiocchi, G. (2012). The power of ambiguity: How participatory budgeting travels the globe. *Journal of Public Deliberation*, **8**(2), 1–12.

García-Guadilla, M. (2008). La praxis de los consejos comunales en Venezuela. *Revista Venezolana de Economía y Ciencias Sociales*, **14**(1), 125–51.

Geissel, B. (2012). Impacts of democratic innovations in Europe: Findings and desiderata. In B. Geissel and K. Newton, eds., *Evaluating Democratic Innovations: Curing the Democratic Malaise?* London: Routledge, 163–83.

Geissel, B. (2013). Introduction: On the Evaluation of Participatory Innovations - A Preliminary Framework. In Geissel, B., & Joas, M. eds. Participatory democratic innovations in Europe: Improving the quality of democracy? Verlag Barbara Budrich.

Goldfrank, B. (2006). Los procesos de "presupuesto participativo" en América Latina: Éxito, fracaso y cambio. *Revista de Ciencia Política (Santiago)*, **26**(2), 3–28.

Goldfrank, B. (2011). *Deepening Local Democracy in Latin America*. Philadelphia: Pennsylvania State University Press.

Goldfrank, B. (2012). The World Bank and the globalization of participatory budgeting. *Journal of Public Deliberation*, **8**(2), 1–18.

Habermas, J. (1996). *Between Facts and Norms*. Cambridge, MA: MIT Press.

Hall, P. A., & Thelen, K. (2009). Institutional change in varieties of capitalism. *Socio-economic review*, **7**(1), 7–34.

Hawkins, K. A. (2010). Who mobilizes? Participatory democracy in Chávez's Bolivarian revolution. *Latin American Politics and Society*, **52**, 31–66.

Heller, P., & Rao, V. (2015). *Deliberation and Development*. Washington, DC: World Bank.

Helmke, G., & Levitsky, S. (2004). Informal institutions and comparative politics: A research agenda. *Perspectives on Politics*, **2**(4), 725–740.

Helvetas & UNICEF. (2018). El primer Programa de Saneamiento Total Liderado por la Comunidad (SANTOLIC) en Guatemala, https://helvetas.org/es/guatemala/quienes-somos/Nuestros%20Proyectos/SAHTOSO.

Hendriks, C. (2016). Coupling citizens and elites in deliberative systems: The role of institutional design. *European Journal of Political Research*, **55**(1), 43–60.

Herrera, V. (2017). From participatory promises to partisan capture: Local democratic transitions and Mexican water politics. *Comparative Politics*, **49**(4), 479–499.

He, B., & Warren, M. E. (2011). Authoritarian Deliberation: The Deliberative Turn in Chinese Political Development. *Perspectives on Politics*, 9(2), 269–289.

Hevia, F. J., & Isunza Vera, E. (2012). Participación acotada: Consejos consultivos e incidencia en políticas públicas en el ámbito federal mexicano. In M. A. Cameron, E. Hershberg and K. E. Sharp, eds., *Nuevas instituciones de democracia participativa en América Latina: La voz y sus consecuencias*. Mexico City: Facultad Latinoamericana de Ciencias Sociales, pp. 105–36.

International IDEA. (2021). Global State of Democracy Report 2021, https://idea.int/democracytracker/sites/default/files/2022-11/GSOD21.pdf.

Jann, W., & Wegrich, K. (2007). Theories of the Policy Cycle. In F. Fischer, G. J. Miller and M. S. Sidney, eds., *Handbook of Public Policy Analysis*. New York: Routledge, 43–62.

Knight, J., & Johnson, J. (2011). *The Priority of Democracy: Political Consequences of Pragmatism*. Princeton NJ: Princeton University Press.

Knill, C., & Tosun, J. (2012). *Public Policy: A New Introduction*. London: Macmillan International Higher Education.

Lagos, M. (2018). El fin de la tercera ola de democracias. Informe Latinobarómetro, https://google.com/url?sa=t&rct=j&q=&esrc=s&source=web&cd=&ved=2ahUKEwii0aewwsL8AhXwQfEDHWq7BGUQFnoECAoQAQ&url=https%3A%2F%2Fwww.latinobarometro.org%2Flatdocs%2FAnnus_Horribilis.pdf&usg=AOvVaw26db200TrRNFTW70cKJ5IG.

Latinobarómetro Corporation. (2021). Latinobarómetro Report 2021, https://latinobarometro.org/latContents.jsp.

Levitsky, S., & Loxton, J. (2013). Populism and competitive authoritarianism in the Andes. *Democratization*, **20**(1), 107–36.

Levitsky, S., & Murillo, M. V. (2009). Variation in institutional strength. *Annual Review of Political Science*, **12**, 115–33.

Lissidini, A. (2010). *Democracia directa en América Latina: Riesgos y oportunidades*. Buenos Aires: Prometeo.

López Maya, M. (2011). Los consejos comunales en Caracas vistos por sus participantes: una exploración. *Política & Sociedad*, **10**(18), 187–222.

Mainwaring, S. (2012). From Representative Democracy to Participatory Competitive Authoritarianism: Hugo Chávez and Venezuelan Politics. *Perspectives on Politics*, 10(4), 955–967.

Mansbridge, J. (2015). A minimalist definition of deliberation. In P. Heller and V. Rao, eds., *Deliberation and Development*. Washington, DC: World Bank, 27–49.

Mansbridge, J., Bohman, J., Chambers., S. et al. (2012). A systemic approach to deliberative democracy. In J. Parkinson and J. Mansbridge, eds., *Deliberative Systems*. Cambridge: Cambridge University Press, 1–26.

Margetts, H., John, P., Hale, S., & Yasseri, T. (2015). *Political Turbulence: How Social Media Shape Collective Action*. Princeton: Princeton University Press.

Mayka, L. (2019). *Building Participatory Institutions in Latin America: Reform Coalitions and Institutional Change*. Cambridge: Cambridge University Press.

McAdam, D., Tarrow S., & Tilly, C. (2001). *The Dynamics of Contention*. New York: Cambridge University Press.

McNulty, S. L. (2019). *Democracy from Above? The Unfulfilled Promise of Nationally Mandated Participatory Reforms*. Stanford: Stanford University Press.

Merkel, W. (2011). Volksabstimmungen: Illusion und Realität. *Aus Politik und Zeitgeschichte*, 44(45), 47–55.

Morlino, L. (2011). *Changes for Democracy: Actors, Structures, Processes*. Oxford: Oxford University Press.

Muntaner, C., Armada, F., Chung, H., et al. (2008). "Barrio Adentro" en Venezuela: Democracia participativa, cooperación sur-sur y salud para todos. Medicina Social, 3(4), 306–22.

Murillo, M. V. (2020). Elections and Protests in Latin America: Covid-19's Impact. *Items, Insights from the Social Science*, https://items.ssrc.org/covid-19-and-the-social-sciences/democracy-and-pandemics/elections-and-pro tests-in-latin-america-covid-19s-impact/.

Murillo, M. V. (2021). Protestas, descontento y democracia en América Latina. *Nueva Sociedad* (294), https://biblat.unam.mx/hevila/Nuevasociedad/2021/ no294/1.pdf.

Noveck, B. S. (2018). CrowdLaw: Collective intelligence and lawmaking. *Analyse & Kritik*, **40**, 359–80.

O'Donnell, G., & Schmitter, P. C. (1986). *Transitions from Authoritarian Rule: Tentative Conclusions about Uncertain Democracies*. Baltimore: Johns Hopkins University.

O'Donnell, G. (1993). On the state, democratization and some conceptual problems: A Latin American view with glances at some postcommunist countries. *World Development*, 21(8), 1355–1369.

O'Donnell, G. (2004). The quality of democracy: Why the rule of law matters. *Journal of Democracy*, 4, 32–46.

OECD. (2020). *Innovative Citizen Participation and New Democratic Institutions: Catching the Deliberative Wave*. Paris: OECD Publishing. https://doi.org/10.1787/339306da-en.

Paredes, J. P. (2011). Ciudadanía, participación y democracia: Deuda y déficit en los 20 años de "democracia" en Chile. *Polis, Revista de la Universidad Bolivariana*, **10**(20), 473–499.

Parkinson, J. (2012). Democratizing deliberative systems. In J. Parkinson and J. Mansbridge, eds., *Deliberative Systems*. Cambridge: Cambridge University Press, 151–72.

Pateman, C. (2012). Participatory democracy revisited. *Perspectives on Politics*, **10**(1), 7–19.

Peixoto, T., & Sifry, M. L. (2017). *Civic Tech in The Global South: Assessing Technology for the Public Good*. Washington, DC: World Bank Personal Democracy Press.

Pitkin, H. F. (1967). *The Concept of Representation*. Berkeley: University of California Press.

Pogrebinschi, T. (2013). *The Pragmatic Turn of Democracy in Latin America*. FES Studies. Berlin: Friedrich-Erbert-Stiftung.

Pogrebinschi, T. (2018). Experimenting with participation and deliberation in Latin America: Is democracy turning pragmatic? In T. Falleti and E. Parrado, eds., *Latin America Since the Left Turn*. Philadelphia: University of Pennsylvania Press, 241–263.

Pogrebinschi, T. (2020). Might social intelligence save Latin America from its governments in times of Covid-19? Open Democracy, https://opendemoc racy.net/en/democraciaabierta/puede-la-inteligencia-social-salvar-a-amer ica-latina-de-sus-gobiernos-en-tiempos-de-covid-en/.

Pogrebinschi, T. (2021a). LATINNO Dataset on Democratic Innovations in Latin America. Version 1.0.0. WZB Berlin Social Science Center. Dataset, DOI: https://doi.org/10.7802/2278.

Pogrebinschi, T. (2021b). *Codebook for the LATINNO Dataset*. Berlin: WZB Berlin Social Science Center.

Pogrebinschi, T. (2021c). *Thirty Years of Democratic Innovations in Latin America*. Berlin: WZB Berlin Social Science Center.

Pogrebinschi, T. & Acosta, F. A. (2023). The Impact of Democratic Innovations in Latin America. In: Jacquet, V., Ryan, M., & van der Does, R. (Eds.). The impact of democratic innovations. Colchester: ECPR Press, 2023.

Pogrebinschi, T., & Ross, M. (2019). Democratic innovations in Latin America. In S. Elstub and O. Escobar, eds., *Handbook of Democratic Innovation and Governance*. Massachusetts, USA: Edward Elgar, 389–403.

Pogrebinschi, T., & Samuels, D. (2014). The impact of participatory democracy: Evidence from Brazil's national public policy conference. *Comparative Politics*, **46**(3), 313–332.

Pogrebinschi, T., & Santos, F. (2011). Participação como representação: O impacto das conferências nacionais de políticas públicas no Congresso Nacional. *Dados*, **54**(3), 259–305.

Pogrebinschi, T., & Tanscheit, T. (2017a). *Moving Backwards: What Happened to Citizen Participation in Brazil?* Open Democracy, https://opendemocracy .net/en/democraciaabierta/moving-backwards-what-happened-to-citizen-part/.

Pogrebinschi, T., & Ventura, T. (2017b). Mais participação, maior responsividade? *Dados*, **60**(1), 7–43.

Rich, J. A., Mayka, L., & Montero, A. P. (2019). The politics of participation in Latin America: New actors and institutions. *Latin American Politics and Society*, **61**(2), 1–20.

Roberts, K. M. (1998). *Deepening Democracy? The Modern Left and Social Movements in Chile and Peru*. Stanford: Stanford University Press.

Roberts, K. M. (2016). (Re)Politicizing inequalities: Movements, parties, and social citizenship in Chile. *Journal of Politics in Latin America*, 8(3), 125–54.

Ryan, M. (2021). *Why Citizen Participation Succeeds or Fails: A Comparative Analysis of Participatory Budgeting*. Bristol: Bristol University Press.

Sartori, G. (1970). Concept misformation in comparative politics. *American Political Science Review*, **64**(4), 1033–53.

Sartori, G. (2009 [1975]). The tower of Babel. In D. Collier and J. Gerring, eds., *Concepts and Method in Social Science: The Tradition of Giovanni Sartori*. London: Routledge, 97–150.

Selee, A., & Peruzzotti, E. (eds.) (2009). *Participatory Innovation and Representative Democracy in Latin America*. Baltimore: Woodrow Wilson Center Press

Smith G. (2009). *Democratic Innovations: Designing Institutions for Citizen Participation*. Cambridge: Cambridge University Press.

Shenk, J. (2022). Comparative Politics, Volume 55, Number 1, October 2022, pp. 1–22(22).

Smith, G. (2019). Reflections on the theory and practice of democratic innovations. In S. Elstub and O. Escobar, eds., *Handbook of Democratic Innovation and Governance*. Cheltenham: Edward Elgar, 572–582.

Spada, P., & Ryan, M. (2017), The failure to examine failures in democratic innovations. *PS: Political Science & Politics*, 50(3), 772–778.

Statista. (2021). *Number of internet users in selected Latin American countries 2021 (in millions)*. Statista Inc. https://statista.com/statistics/186919/num ber-of-internet-users-in-latin-american-countries/.

Strandberg, K., & Grönlund, K. (2018). Online deliberation. In : A. Bächtiger, J. S. Dryzek, J. Mansbridge and M. E. Warren, eds., *The Oxford Handbook of Deliberative Democracy*. Oxford: Oxford University Press, 365–377.

Tapia, A. and M. Hernandez (2016). La situación de los defensores de Derechos Humanos en Colombia. *Cuadernos Deusto de Derechos Humanos*, **82**.

Touchton, M., & Wampler, B. (2014). Improving social well-being through new democratic institutions. *Comparative Political Studies*, **47**(10), 1442–1469.

UNDP Honduras. (2019). Avances en municipios con los Observatorios Municipales de Convivencia y Seguridad Ciudadana (OMCSC). Retrieved from www.hn.undp.org/content/honduras/es/home/library/infosegura/avances-en-municipios-con-los-observatorios-municipales-de-convi.html.

UNDP. (2009). Guatemala: hacia un estado para el desarollo humano. Informe nacional de desarrollo humano 2009/2010. desarrollohumano.org.gt/biblio teca/informes-nacionales/.

UNDP. (2014). Devolución del Diálogo Nacional sobre VIH y el derecho: Un proceso participativo de consulta sobre los retos en Guatemala.

Unger, R. (1998). *Democracy Realized*. London: Verso.

Urbinati, N., & Warren, M. E. (2008). The concept of representation in contemporary democratic theory. *Annual Review of Political Science*, **11**, 387–412.

Velásquez, F. E. (2011). La institucionalización de la participación en Colombia. *Política & Sociedade*, **10**(18), 155–186.

von Bülow, M., & Donoso, S. (2017). Introduction: Social movements in contemporary Chile. In S. Donoso and M. von Bülow, eds., *Social Movements in Chile: Organization, Trajectories, and Political Consequences*. New York: Palgrave Macmillan, 3–28.

Wampler, B. (2007). *Participatory Budgeting in Brazil: Contestation, Cooperation, and Accountability*. University Park: Penn State University Press.

Wampler, B., & Goldfrank, B. (2022). *The Rise, Spread, and Decline of Brazil's Participatory Budgeting. The Arc of a Democratic Innovation*, Cham, Switzerland: Palgrave Macmillan.

Wampler, B., McNulty, S., & Touchton, M. (2021). *Participatory Budgeting in Global Perspective*. New York, NY: Oxford University Press.

Wampler, B., Sugiyama, N. B., & Touchton, M. (2019). *Democracy at Work: Pathways to Well-Being in Brazil*. Cambridge: Cambridge University Press.

Warren, M. E. (2008). Citizen representatives. In M. Warren and H. Pearse, eds., *Designing Deliberative Democracy: The British Columbia Citizens' Assembly*. Cambridge: Cambridge University Press, 50–69.

Warren, M. E. (2009). Governance driven democratization. *Critical Policy Studies*, **3**(3), 3–13.

Warren, M. E. (2017). A Problem-based approach to democratic theory. *American Political Science Review*, 111.

Welp, Y. (2018). Recall referendum around the world. In L. Morel and M. Qvortrup, eds., *The Routledge Handbook to Referendums and Direct Democracy*. New York: Routledge, 451–463.

Zaremberg, G., Guarneros-Meza, V., & Lavalle, A. G. (2017). *Intermediation and Representation in Latin America*. London: Palgrave Macmillan.

Acknowledgments

Several great people and institutions have been crucial in the process that culminated with this Element. The WZB Berlin Social Science Center, which offers me the best possible conditions to do research; The Open Society Foundations, which made my LATINNO project possible; The Ash Center at Harvard University, where I started to write the initial ideas. Big thanks to my LATINNO team, and especially Fátima Ávila Acosta, Melisa Ross, and Gisella Vogel for research assistance. For various essential exchanges, many thanks to Archon Fung, Jane Mansbridge, Wolfgang Merkel, Leonardo Morlino, Brian Wampler, Mark Warren, and Bernhard Wessels. Specials thanks to Scott Mainwaring for the motivation in the early stages of writing and to Ernesto Ganuza for the encouragement until the last revision. I am highly indebted to Tulia Falleti for the invitation to write this Element and for enabling me to greatly improve it. Thanks also to the anonymous reviewers for their valuable comments and suggestions. Finally, I dedicate this work to my daughter Hannah, so she never forgets that women can be and do anything they wish, and that I love her beyond the infinite.

Cambridge Elements ≡

Politics and Society in Latin America

Maria Victoria Murillo
Columbia University

Maria Victoria Murillo is Professor of Political Science and International Affairs at Columbia University. She is the author of *Political Competition, Partisanship, and Policymaking in the Reform of Latin American Public Utilities* (Cambridge, 2009). She is also editor of *Carreras Magisteriales, Desempeño Educativo y Sindicatos de Maestros en América Latina* (2003), and co-editor of *Argentine Democracy: the Politics of Institutional Weakness* (2005). She has published in edited volumes as well as in the *American Journal of Political Science, World Politics*, and *Comparative Political Studies*, among others.

Tulia G. Falleti
University of Pennsylvania

Tulia G. Falleti is the Class of 1965 Endowed Term Professor of Political Science, Director of the Latin American and Latino Studies Program, and Senior Fellow of the Leonard Davis Institute for Health Economics at the University of Pennsylvania. She received her BA in Sociology from the Universidad de Buenos Aires and her Ph.D. in Political Science from Northwestern University. Falleti is the author of *Decentralization and Subnational Politics in Latin America* (Cambridge University Press, 2010), which earned the Donna Lee Van Cott Award for best book on political institutions from the Latin American Studies Association, and with Santiago Cunial of *Participation in Social Policy: Public Health in Comparative Perspective* (Cambridge University Press, 2018). She is co-editor, with Orfeo Fioretos and Adam Sheingate, of *The Oxford Handbook of Historical Institutionalism* (Oxford University Press, 2016), among other edited books. Her articles on decentralization, federalism, authoritarianism, and qualitative methods have appeared in edited volumes and journals such as the *American Political Science Review, Comparative Political Studies, Publius, Studies in Comparative International Development*, and *Qualitative Sociology*, among others.

Juan Pablo Luna
The Pontifical Catholic University of Chile

Juan Pablo Luna is Professor of Political Science at The Pontifical Catholic University of Chile. He received his BA in Applied Social Sciences from the UCUDAL (Uruguay) and his PhD in Political Science from the University of North Carolina at Chapel Hill. He is the author of *Segmented Representation. Political Party Strategies in Unequal Democracies* (Oxford University Press, 2014), and has co-authored *Latin American Party Systems* (Cambridge University Press, 2010). In 2014, along with Cristobal Rovira, he co-edited *The Resilience of the Latin American Right* (Johns Hopkins University). His work on political representation, state capacity, and organized crime has appeared in the following journals: *Comparative Political Studies, Revista de Ciencia Política, the Journal of Latin American Studies, Latin American Politics and Society, Studies in Comparative International Development, Política y Gobierno, Democratization, Perfiles Latinoamericanos*, and the *Journal of Democracy*.

Andrew Schrank
Brown University

Andrew Schrank is the Olive C. Watson Professor of Sociology and International & Public Affairs at Brown University. He received his BA from the University of Michigan He received his BA from the University of Michigan and his PhD from the University of Wisconsin. His articles on business, labor, and the state in Latin America have appeared in the *American Journal of Sociology, Comparative Politics, Comparative Political Studies, Latin American Politics & Society, Social Forces*, and *World Development*, among other journals, and his co-authored book, *Root-Cause Regulation: Labor Inspection in Europe and the Americas,* is forthcoming at Harvard University Press.

Advisory Board
Javier Auyero, *University of Texas at Austin*
Daniela Campello, *Fundação Getúlio Vargas*
Eduardo Dargent, *Universidad Catolica, Peru*
Alberto Diaz-Cayeros, *Stanford University*
Kathy Hoschtetler, *London School of Economics*
Evelyne Huber, *University of North Carolina, Chapel Hill*
Robert Kaufman, *Rutgers University*
Steven Levitsky, *Harvard University*
Antonio Lucero, *University of Washington, Seattle*
Juliana Martinez, *Universidad de Costa Rica*
Alfred P. Montero, *Carlton College*
Alison Post, *University of California, Berkeley*
Gabriel Vommaro, *Universidad Nacional de General Sarmiento*
Deborah Yashar, *Princeton University*
Gisela Zaremberg, *Flacso México*
Veronica Zubilaga, *Universidad Simon Boliviar*

About the Series
Latin American politics and society are at a crossroads, simultaneously confronting serious challenges and remarkable opportunities that are likely to be shaped by formal institutions and informal practices alike. The Elements series on Politics and Society in Latin America offers multidisciplinary and methodologically pluralist contributions on the most important topics and problems confronted by the region

Cambridge Elements ≡

Politics and Society in Latin America

A full series listing is available at: www.cambridge.org/PSLT